"John Watkis is a unique and innovative leader who has been able to share his gifts on some of the top stages as Mufasa in *The Lion King*. Just as he played the Lion King, he now teaches others how to bring out the regal aspects of their talents and become the King or Queen of their stages. Listen to him, learn from him, and let him help you to grow the greatness that you have inside of you!"

Dr. Willie Jolley
Hall of Fame Speaker and Best-Selling Author of
A Setback Is A Setup For A Comeback,
and An Attitude of Excellence

SPEAKING NOTES

The Eight Essential Elements to Make
Your Speech Music to Their Ears

JOHN WATKIS

ISBN: 9781079546019 (paperback)

Independently Published
www.johnwatkis.com

SPEAKING NOTES

Christina,

May your words be music to
the ears of all who hear you speak.

JWatkins

In memory of my grandmother,
Mommy G (Violet Stoddart)

This book is dedicated to my sons, Joshua
and Jordan, whose voices and laughter
have always been music to my ears.

CONTENTS

ACKNOWLEDGEMENTS

It's hard to believe this book could possibly have taken longer to write. After all, I started writing it 10 years ago and still didn't manage to finish it by the original deadline listed in my presale. But the book would have taken longer (and possibly never been finished) if it weren't for the encouragement (and occasional butt kicking) of some friends and colleagues who refused to let me forget I had a book to get out into the world.

Celia Beamish, who has been a huge supporter in my professional endeavors. Your critical eye and push for perfection made the content in this book so much better. Thank you for challenging me to dig deeper and create something I can be proud of. I appreciate the weekly text messages and phone calls urging me to get this done.

Betty Norlin, my accountability partner, encourager, guardian angel, and editor of my second draft. I appreciate you more than words can say. Thank you for allowing me to move past the frustrating moments of writing while still holding my feet to the fire. I can't thank you enough.

To my mastermind group: Dr. Pat Baxter, Sherril Harris, and David Prosper. Even when you knew there were better ways to work through the process, you supported me and challenged me every step of the way. I couldn't ask for better partners and coaches.

Marsha Lawrence, my Canadian friend and emergency editor who found time in her busy schedule to get my chapters back to me lickity split. You've been there for me through so many phases of my life and have many stories about me you could share with the world. Thank you for keeping them to yourself!

Carolyn Quintin, my Dean in the National Speakers Association Central Florida chapter Speakers Academy, who was my accountability partner when I needed to get my first draft finished. Thank you for being a constant encourager and idea generator. I appreciate all you do for me and others who aspire to grow their speaking businesses.

Deb Cheslow. This book was dead and forgotten until I took your coaching program. Your powerful coaching and tools taught me to dream again and do things I no longer believed were in reach.

Allison Shapira, Founder and CEO of Global Public Speaking. You are a source of inspiration for me and I'm honored to be part of your team. Thank you for the conversations and encouragement to get my work out into the world.

Meghan Gonzalez, Director of Client Experience at Global Public Speaking. Thank you for lending your ear and offering timely suggestions and solutions during the 11th hour. I appreciate your ability to offer clarity when it came down to crunch time.

To all those who made advance purchases of my book and waited patiently (or forgot) when the deadline came and went:

Aarti Koilpillai
Marly Sayler
Holly Pearson
Claudia Virga

Phil Gerbyshak

Susan Urban

Ana Gonzalez

Brian Reeves

Angela Mitchell

Lisa Demmi

Kate Holgate

Shari Bruno

Maya Horvathova

Kathleen Pope

Karen Burke

Michele Neray

Diane Gibson

Karen Warren

Kelley Dameo

Carolyn Quintin

Angela McIntosh

Dr. Pat Baxter

Jonathan Rotenberg

Getting permission to use material from books and speeches takes far more effort and research than most people would imagine. Michael E. Eidenmuller, from AmericanRhetoric.com, and Mark Pearson, from Pear Press, responded to me immediately and saved me a lot of legwork.

Thank you to Freepik, at Flaticon.com, for creating the musical icons used throughout the book.

Finally, a huge shout out to my final draft editor, Liz Coursen. She's the only person in this section who added more time to getting this book done, but it was with good cause. Liz encouraged (twisted my arm?) me to add more personal stories so you, the reader, could get insights into who I am and how I use the principles I discuss in the book. It was a challenging process, but one I'm glad she convinced me to work through.

INTRODUCTION

"P.S. I've been meaning to ask you. Do you play any musical instruments?"

The question at the end of my client's email came straight out of left field.

I had written a speech for her and she was following up to give me feedback and let me know how much the audience members loved it.

As a speechwriter, I love to receive that type of feedback. Quite frankly, it never gets old. Her "P.S.," however, had me puzzled. It had nothing to do with anything we had previously discussed.

Why would she want to know that? I thought to myself.

After congratulating her on a job well done, I sought to satisfy my curiosity.

I had to know...why did she want to know if I played a musical instrument?

This was her response:

The reason I ask is because a tip I learned a long time ago was... when you're looking for a great speechwriter, and I can quote, "Do yourself a favor and first ask whether he or she is musical at all. Find out if they play any kind of instrument. or sing."

She went on to say that *the* best speechwriters all have some musical talent. Because...a speech is made to be listened to so it has to have rhythm. Quiet parts and then crescendos.

Changes in pitch and pace and overall structure and shape. A speech has to have words that are easy to say and clear to be understood and appreciated by those listening to it.

In essence...the best speechwriters write for the ear.

And—when I read your final product (in terms of the speech), I felt it had these things. And I actually mentioned to my husband at the time, "I'll bet John is musical in some way." So—I kept meaning to ask, but forgot. I guess you could say I was checking the theory. Not sure if you've heard similar comparisons to musical and writing talents...but there's the comparison.

What do ya think?

I wasn't sure what I thought, but I was fascinated by the possibility. You see...I'm not just musical in "some way"...music is in my blood.

My grandmother, "Mommy G," played the harmonica (which she referred to as the "mouth organ") up until she passed away at the age of 99 years, 360 days. In her nineties, she would visit nursing homes and, according to her, "play for the old people."

My Aunt Dawn plays the piano. My Uncle Garfield plays the guitar, electric bass, and the keyboards. As a teenager, I spent weekends in his bedroom creating cassette tapes from the wall-to-wall collection of vinyl records he still owns to this day.

My mother sang alto in her church choir and always had music playing in our home. We had a massive wooden stereo unit that housed both a record player and an 8-track cassette player that made clunking sounds as you switched between tracks. I can still hear the sounds of Percy Sledge, Stevie Wonder, Kenny Rogers, Boney M., and Disco Duck.

My mother also enrolled me in multiple lessons when I was a child: tap, jazz, piano...music was always present in my life in some way, shape, or form.

In middle school, I played the tenor saxophone (more on that later) and fell in love with the idea of being a performer. I spent countless hours singing and dancing in front of a full-length mirror singing the songs of New Edition and imagining I was performing for sellout crowds.

When I made the transition to high school, I attended Claude Watson School of the Arts. It was the Canadian equivalent of the hit show "Fame" that I watched on a weekly basis. I majored in theater arts and took minors in music and dance. I was reunited with the piano and took a greater interest in exploring my musical gifts. Incidentally, it was also a time in my life when my body and voice were changing dramatically and I hadn't quite made the adjustment to facilitate all those changes. As a result, I failed in a number of areas.

I failed to make the school musical *The Pajama Game*.

I failed to make it as part of the Jazz Choir.

I failed to make it into the school talent show with future *Soul Train* and *Juno* award-winner Deborah Cox (she got in performing a solo).

If there was ever a reason to question my musical talents, I had sufficient proof I couldn't cut it.

But as the changes in my voice and body began to slow down, I started to experience more success.

When I joined the church at age 18, I immediately auditioned for what was then the 110-voice Association of Gospel Music Ministries Mass Choir. It would eventually get smaller and was renamed "Toronto Mass Choir" under the direction of Karen Burke. I would go on to become Karen's assistant choir director.

The Pentecostal churches I attended were very close to what you might see in a movie. The preachers didn't just speak...they sang their sermons. Musicians emphasized key phrases and added background accompaniment to match the mood of the moment. I would eventually lead song services in the capacity of "Praise & Worship" leader.

In 2000, my life became totally immersed in music when I was cast as a member of the singing ensemble and as the understudy for Mufasa in the original Toronto cast of *The Lion King* musical.

After leaving *The Lion King*, I began learning Latin dancing and went on to win a salsa competition with my then partner.

I had never connected any of my performing background with my method for writing speeches until my client "popped the question." But, as I reflected on my experience onstage, I wondered...had I been using my musical talents to write speeches all along?

I wasn't sure, because, when it came to writing speeches, I hadn't examined how I did what I did. I just did it. I was what you might call an "unconscious competent." But now I was curious:

Was there really a connection between musicality and successful speeches?

I had to find out.

I scoured the internet in search of articles, research papers, books, videos…any information that connected the two. But my search turned up little…*very* little.

Rather than looking for information connecting the two, I chose a different approach. I researched the two subjects individually.

I researched information on how to write songs. I interviewed musicians. I dusted off my old music books and reacquainted myself with music theory.

Then I studied the composition of some of the most memorable speeches in history. Speeches such as

"I have a dream"

"We shall fight on the beaches"

"Ask not what your country can do for you"

Once I brought my research together, I was amazed by what I had discovered. There was, indeed, a connection between music and successful speeches. Not only was there a connection between music and speeches, there were Eight Essential Elements that made speeches sound like music to the ears. The Eight Essential Elements can be used by anyone, even if he or she doesn't have musical talent or knowledge of music theory.

That's what I'll be sharing with you throughout this book…how to use the Eight Essential Elements of music in your speeches.

Whether you're a politician, professional speaker, CEO, consultant, team leader, communications specialist, world-class athlete, student, preacher, teacher, or entrepreneur, this book will show you how to develop and deliver speeches that will improve your powers of persuasion, build your reputation, and move your audience members to take action.

Whether you write speeches or deliver them…whether you are new to giving speeches or experienced…once you learn how to weave the Eight Essential Elements of music into your speeches, audiences will say your speech was music to their ears.

Are you ready to make beautiful music together?

Good. Music, Maestro!

THE EIGHT
ESSENTIAL ELEMENTS

*B*efore we jump into discussing the Eight Essential Elements of music that exist in successful speeches, let's set the standard for a successful speech.

I've boiled the criteria down to three effects both music and successful speeches have on the people who listen to them.

EFFECT #1
Music and successful speeches are easy to *remember*.

Depending on your age, I'm willing to bet you can remember songs, word for word, you haven't heard in 10, 20...maybe even 50 years. I'm also willing to bet you can remember signature stories, analogies, and phrases you heard in speeches several decades ago. This doesn't happen by mistake. Both music and successful speeches are structured so it's easy for the listener to remember them.

EFFECT #2
Music and successful speeches are *repeated* by those who hear them.

Have you ever heard a song you liked so much, you couldn't help but tell a friend about it? Have you ever heard a song on the radio and then caught yourself singing the song? Have you ever found yourself singing a song you couldn't stand? My answer to all of those questions is a resounding "Yes!" The same is true of successful speeches. Have you ever repeated the phrases "I have a dream," "Ask not what your country can do for you," "The only thing to fear is fear itself," or, more recently, "Yes we can"? It's not a coincidence. Both music and successful speeches are structured in such a way that listeners will repeat their words.

EFFECT #3
Music and successful speeches are *responded* to by their listeners.

If you're the type who enjoys people watching, you've probably seen what I refer to as "karaoke shopping stars." These are your run-of-the-mill adults who saunter down the dairy aisle and break into song and dance when one of their favorite oldies starts to play over the P.A. system. Without giving it a second thought, they end up *responding* to the music. I highly doubt a speech will ever cause someone to dance in the dairy aisle, but people *respond* to successful speeches.

They *respond* by donating to charities.

They *respond* by casting their votes.

They *respond* by increasing their productivity at work.

Once again, this isn't a coincidence, because music and successful speeches are crafted so people will respond to them.

Notice there was no mention of a standing ovation, 10 out of 10 on evaluation forms, or compliments from members of the audience when they pass you in the hallway. While those are all nice for your ego, that type of feedback doesn't tell you whether or not your speech was successful.

The standard for a successful speech is that your audience *remembers, repeats,* and *responds* to it.

THE EIGHT ESSENTIAL ELEMENTS

Now that we've set the standard for a successful speech, let's do a quick overview of the Eight Essential Elements that make a speech sound like music to the ears of your audience members.

Element #1: The Chorus

In music, the chorus is the central theme of the song. The chorus is the reason the song was written. In your speech, the chorus is the theme or main point of your speech. The chorus is your reason for delivering the speech.

Element #2: The Hook

In music, the hook is the catchy part of a song (it may exist in the chorus) that you can't get out of your head. It's the part that people sing to themselves over and over. In your speech, the hook is the word, phrase, or sentence that people remember and repeat long after your speech has been given.

Element #3: Verses

In music, the verses of a song help you to better understand the chorus. They tell the whole story behind the chorus. In a speech, your verses will have the same role: to bring clarity to the chorus and tell your story.

Element #4: Pre-Chorus

The pre-chorus indicates you are making a transition from one part of your song to the next. In speeches, your pre-chorus serves as a point of transition from one thought to another or one section to another.

Element #5: Mood

In music, every song creates a mood. People often listen to music to get into a mood or get out of a mood. The mood is set at the start of the song. In speeches, you also have to set a mood that is appropriate for the audience and the occasion.

Element #6: Rhythm

In music, rhythm is the variation of the duration of sounds (notes) within a certain time frame. In speech, rhythm is the variation of word length and sentence structure.

Element #7: Expression

In music, expression marks are used to describe how notes are to be played: soft, loud, with feeling, etc.

In a speech, expression describes how much or how little emphasis you give to specific words and/or phrases.

Element #8: Bridge

In music, a bridge serves as a point of transition that signals the end of the song is near. The transition usually takes the song to a higher level of emotion before "connecting" back to the chorus. In a speech, the bridge is used to reflect on the speech and then segue into the final chorus.

That's it!

Okay...not exactly. Knowing what the Eight Essential Elements are doesn't mean you know how to weave the elements into your speeches so your words blend together to create perfect harmony.

In the following chapters, I'll break the Eight Essential Elements down, one at a time, and show you how to use them when you develop and deliver your next speech.

If you're working on a speech right now, do the exercises at the end of each chapter to see if you're striking the right chord.

If you haven't started working on a speech, do the exercises at the end of each chapter and you'll have a masterpiece (or something close) when you're finished.

Regardless of why you're reading the book, do the exercises at the end of each chapter so this book doesn't become another good read you put on the shelf and forget.

Speaking Notes: The Eight Essential Elements to Make Your Speech Music to Their Ears is meant to be a guide and resource you use every time you prepare a speech of any kind.

On that note, let's get started with Essential Element #1, the Chorus.

ESSENTIAL ELEMENT 1:
THE CHORUS

"It's my party and..."

"It was an itsy-bitsy-teenie-weenie..."

"You ain't nothin' but a..."

How long did it take you to figure out the rest of the words to those choruses? No time at all, right? And you probably haven't heard or thought about those songs in ages!

Why is that? Why are we able to remember the words to choruses we haven't heard for decades?

Here's why...

The chorus is what a song is all about. It's the main message. It's the central theme. And everything in a song revolves around and points to the chorus. But there's more to it. Because the chorus is the central theme in a song, it's repeated over and over and over again...that's why we remember it.

In the same way a song has a chorus, your speech should have a chorus that serves the same purpose. That chorus should be what the speech is all about. It should be the main message. It should be the central theme...and the chorus of your speech should be repeated over and over and over again.

But how do you decide what your chorus is? And how do you develop it?

In music, a chorus is generally made up of two or more lines. In a speech, the chorus is made up of one word, phrase, or sentence.

In order to decide what that word, phrase, or sentence will be, you'll need to define the purpose of your speech first.

First, what do *you* want to do?

Do you want to inform your audience members?

Do you want to inspire them?

Do you want to demonstrate something to them?

Do you want to persuade them?

You may want to do one of the four, or you may want to do a combination. That's the first half of defining your purpose. Consider it the "what" part of your purpose. It defines "what" you want to do during the speech.

The second half of defining your purpose can be considered the "why": "Why" are you informing, inspiring, demonstrating, or persuading?

After all, you're informing your listeners so they can use the information in a specific way...what way? And if you're inspiring them, you're inspiring them to do something...but what?

To get a better grip on the "why," think about this for a moment... When you're delivering your speech, what do you want your audience to think and feel?

And when you've finished delivering your speech, what do you want your audience to do?

The answers to those questions will be your "why."

Once you've clearly answered the "what" and "why" questions, you'll have a compass to guide you through your speech. This compass will determine the stories you tell, the examples you use, and the quotations you include. It will also determine what you exclude. If the examples, stories, or statistics don't help move you closer to achieving the purpose of your speech, don't use them.

Here are two examples of speeches meant to inform and persuade.

Example 1:

The purpose of my speech is to inform our supporters of how their donations have been used over the past year by our charity. I also want to persuade them to continue donating to our charity again this year.

I want them to feel satisfied their donations have been put to good use. At the end of the presentation, I want them to make a commitment to donate more to our charity.

Example 2:

The purpose of my speech is to inform our staff of the changes our organization will experience over the next few months and to persuade team members to prepare for the upcoming changes.

I want the staff members to think the changes we will be facing are manageable changes, and I want them to feel the organization will be supportive of them as they go through a learning curve.

At the end of the presentation, I want staff members to start charting a plan for how they can best handle the changes. And I want them to share that plan with their managers and directors. Neither of the examples above would be considered your chorus, because, as you'll recall, your chorus should be one word, phrase, or sentence. To get to your chorus, boil your purpose statement down.

For example, the chorus for the first example could be "your giving has helped." It could also be "we couldn't have done this without you."

The chorus for the second example could be as simple as "the coming changes," "here we grow again," or "change: the constant challenge."

Whatever you decide, your chorus needs to be woven throughout the entire speech. There are a number of different ways to do this. Some methods are more effective than others, but all of them can work if used properly. Use them the wrong way, and you'll quickly hit a sour note.

METHODS OF INCORPORATING THE CHORUS INTO YOUR SPEECH

The methods we'll be discussing to weave your chorus throughout your entire speech are

- Acronym
- Lists
- Analogy
- Repetition

Acronym

One of the more popular methods of weaving a chorus into a speech is by using an acronym. You've probably seen or heard countless variations of this method.

If you've ever listened to a speech on goal setting, it's likely you've been exposed to the "S.M.A.R.T" acronym:

Specific **M**easurable **A**ction-oriented **R**ealistic **T**imeline

It can be a clever technique, but one you have to be careful with.

Here's why...your audience members need to remember what every letter of your acronym means. If you're using a long acronym, or one that's not already embedded in the minds of the audience members, they'll likely forget what some letters mean as you get further into your speech. They may even forget the letters!

Using the S.MA.R.T. acronym as an example, the audience may forget what the "S" stands for by the time you get to the "R." This is one major difference between the written and spoken word. Your listeners can't go back and review the last letter of your acronym the way they could if they were reading a book. The acronym has to be either short or one they're already familiar with. Acronyms can work as the theme for a speech, but they are fraught with challenges. I prefer to use acronyms for specific ideas *within* a speech, but you may find they work quite well as the chorus for your speech.

Lists

Another method of weaving the chorus throughout your speech is by using a list, such as "The Seven Deadly Sins of Public Speaking."

This is another method you have to be careful with. Here's why. The original "Seven Deadly Sins" are:

Pride

Envy

Wrath

Sloth

Avarice

Gluttony

Lust

If your audience members aren't already familiar with the list of sins, you're automatically putting them at a disadvantage by making them learn the list of sins *and* connecting it to the material you're going to teach them. Not only that, if you're going to use "The Seven Deadly Sins" as your theme, you can't make up your own sins. Your main points have to somehow parallel pride, envy, wrath, avarice, gluttony, and lust. If they don't, you end up confusing the audience members who do know the "Seven Deadly Sins," especially if, for example, they think of "avarice" as "greed." In effect, they'll have to forget what they already know, replace existing knowledge with the new list you've made up, *and* remember it all. That's too much work!

The first "R" of a successful speech is "Remember." If you're going to use a list, make sure it's one the audience will be able to *remember* after the speech is finished.

Analogy

A popular, time-tested method of driving home your theme is using an analogy...or comparing your topic with something else the audience is familiar with. Take a look at most of the sermons Jesus taught, and you'll notice his fondness for using analogies to drive his points home. His analogies were referred to as "parables."

Even movies and T.V. shows can be used as analogies. If you plan on using this method, you have to remember a portion of your audience may know of the movie or show, but has never watched it. In that case, you'll have to give a brief overview of the show that will quickly put all listeners on the same page.

I once did this with a presentation I delivered on the topic of customer service. The title of the presentation was "Customer Service Survival Skills." The theme was taken from the reality television show *Survivor.*

In the speech, I compared the three keys to winning on the show with the three keys to winning the customer service "game." My three main keys to becoming a customer service survivor were

1. Building alliances
2. Sharpening your survival skills
3. Winning the immunity challenges

If you're familiar with the show, the three keys will make perfect sense to you.

If you're not familiar with the show, watching one episode would immediately clear it up.

Repetition

The final method for weaving the chorus throughout your speech—and which I consider to be the most effective method—is repetition.

If you want your audience to walk away remembering and repeating your speech, make sure you repeat the chorus as often as possible.

There are a number of examples of using repetition to drive home your theme. The one I'll share with you is from Martin Luther King Jr.'s "I Have a Dream" speech. King began the speech by saying:

> I'm happy to join with you today in what will go down in history as the greatest demonstration for freedom in the history of our nation.

He went on to say the words *free, freedom,* or *liberty* over 30 times in just under 17 minutes. The last words of his speech were

> Free at last, free at last, thank God almighty, we're free at last!

Just as King did in his speech, you should find ways to repeat the word, phrase, or sentence that is the chorus of your speech.

Whatever method you choose, your goal will be to make it easy for your audience members to clearly identify and remember your chorus even if they haven't heard or thought about it for a long time.

EXERCISE: CREATING THE CHORUS

It's time to put theory into practice. Use the following exercises to pinpoint the chorus for your speech.

The Purpose Statement

Using the examples from this chapter, list your goal(s) for this speech.

_____

_____

_____

My purpose for giving this speech is to:

_____

_____

_____

While I'm giving the speech, I want the audience to think:

_____

_____

_____

And I want them to feel:

_____

_____

_____

_____

After the speech, I want the audience to (do):

_____

_____

_____

_____

The Chorus

Brainstorm as many words, phrases, and sentences as you can. Write down everything that comes to mind. *After* you have finished brainstorming, evaluate each idea and pick the one that will be your chorus.

In the next chapter, we'll discuss Essential Element #2, the Hook.

ESSENTIAL ELEMENT 2:
THE HOOK

Even though the chorus is the central theme of a song, it isn't always the most memorable or popular part of a song. The most popular part of a song is called the "hook."

According to music professor John Covach, a hook is "meant to catch the ear of the listener." While the hook is sometimes a part of the chorus, it doesn't always work out that way. For example,

In "The Lion Sleeps Tonight," the hook is

> a-weem-o-weh, a-weem-o-weh, a-weem-o-weh,
> a-weem-o-weh

In "Lady Marmalade," the hook is

> Voulez-vous couchez avec moi, ce soir?

Even though many people have no clue what the last hook means—and even though many people don't know the name of the song or who sings it, toes start tapping and heads begin bobbing whenever and wherever it's played.

Why? Because it's *catchy*.

In the same way good music has a catchy hook, so does a successful speech. Here are a few hooks you may be familiar with:

"Ask not what your country can do for you; ask what you can do for your country."

—John F. Kennedy

"Give me liberty or give me death!"

—Patrick Henry

"I have a dream!"

—Martin Luther King, Jr.

"Read my lips: no new taxes!"

—George H. W. Bush

"If the glove doesn't fit, you must acquit."

—Johnny Cochrane

As was the case with the choruses in the last chapter, I'm sure the hooks were still fresh in your memory. But again, why?

What is it about these hooks that cause them to stay in your head? And how can you create hooks in your speeches?

Good questions.

The "why" of making hooks work isn't as important as the "how." With that in mind, I'll show you how to create similar hooks in your speeches.

When you use one—or a combination—of the following devices, you will create hooks that will be remembered and repeated:

- Antithesis
- Alliteration
- Lists of three
- Repetition
- Emotionally charged words and phrases
- Rhymes

1. ANTITHESIS

Antithesis is the use of two contrasting words, phrases, or ideas directly opposite one another. Two of the hooks I've already mentioned used antithesis:

> "Ask not what your country can do for you. Ask what you can do for your country."

> "Give me liberty or give me death."

People use antithesis in daily conversations without giving it a second thought. You might say things like

"Do or die."

"Now or never."

"It's neither here nor there."

In his book *A Tale of Two Cities,* Charles Dickens created a hook you've heard many times. Most people are familiar with the first set of contrasting phrases, but I've included the whole passage to give you an idea of how effective it can be when you sprinkle your speech with antithesis.

> It was the best of times, it was the worst of times; it was the age of wisdom, it was the age of foolishness; it was the epoch of belief, it was the epoch of incredulity; it was the season of Light, it was the season of Darkness; it was the spring of hope, it was the winter of despair; we had everything before us, we had nothing before us; we were all going direct to Heaven, we were all going direct the other way.

There's another reason I included the whole passage from Dickens. Even if you've read *A Tale of Two Cities* before, it's likely you only remembered the first instance of antithesis. If you want that hook to sink in, put the most powerful phrase first, or use the phrase on its own.

2. ALLITERATION

Alliteration is the repetition of consonant sounds in neighboring words or syllables.

Notice two of the hooks I used for examples of antithesis—"do or die" and "now or never"—are also examples of alliteration. If you're creative enough to come up with phrases that combine both rhetorical devices, your chances of creating a successful hook increase.

You may have noticed the hook I've used for this book includes alliteration. In the first chapter, I wrote:

> "A successful speech is one your audience remembers, repeats, and responds to."

I could have used different words, but none would have been as memorable as the three "R's." Whenever people recap my presentation, those words are always quoted.

Although I only quoted one line from Dr. King's "I Have a Dream" speech, the most popular hook is quite long. The most oft-repeated phrase from King's speech is

> I have a dream...that my four little children will one day live in a nation where they will not be judged by the color of their skin but by the content of their character.

Notice the repetition of the "K" sound:

> Color...skin...content...character.

And did you happen to notice King also used antithesis?

"Not be judged by...but by…"

I'm going to keep reminding you of this powerful principle: When you combine rhetorical devices, your chances of creating a successful hook increase.

3. LISTS OF THREE

Although there are different names for it—"triad" or "lists of three"— the device is still the same...and so are the results. Using a list of three words or phrases in succession is a time-tested technique for creating memorable hooks.

Lists of three that are imbedded in people's brains are:

Of the people,
by the people,
for the people.

Life,
liberty,
and the pursuit of happiness.

I came
I saw
I conquered

Father
Son
Holy Ghost

Faith
Hope
Love

Speaking in lists of threes is memorable. Using a list of two or four doesn't have the same effect. For example, Winston Churchill has often been quoted as saying:

"I have nothing to offer but blood, sweat, and tears."

What he actually said was:

"I have nothing to offer but blood, toil, tears, and sweat."

Still, people only quote three of the four things he stated. Again, speaking in threes is more effective and it's great for creating a hook.

I'm sure you already know I'm going to tell you that when you combine rhetorical devices, your chances of creating a successful hook increase. Let me give you examples of some combinations.

The hook for this book combines alliteration and a list of three:

Remember
Repeat
Respond

A great example of antithesis combined with a list of three comes—
again—from Winston Churchill.

He said:

"Never in the field of human conflict has so much
    been owed by so many to so few."

You get the idea.

When I write my speeches, I leave space for lists of three. If I only
come up with two words or phrases, I leave a "?" in the space and
work on a different section of the speech. I let my subconscious mind
work on filling in the blank, and then I return to it later.

4. REPETITION

In the last chapter, I wrote that one of the most effective ways to
weave your chorus into your speech is to repeat the chorus throughout. As with a chorus, it's also possible to create a hook in your
speech by using repetition. You can repeat the hook at key points
within your speech or in successive sentences.

Key Points

One of my favorite movies of all time is *Back to the Future,* starring
Michael J. Fox. The creativity of the writers and their ability to link
history to the events and culture of 1985 was a thing of beauty. So
when I had the opportunity to help a client write a speech on the
topic of future trends, I seized the opportunity to slip in a *Back to
the Future* reference as a hook.

If you're not familiar with the movie, I'll briefly explain the plot.

30

Marty McFly, the main character played by Fox, travels back in time using a Delorean time machine created by his eccentric friend, Doctor Emmet Brown (Doc). During his time in the past, Marty ends up meeting with younger versions of his mother and father. In the process, he interferes with the events that lead to their first kiss. Much to his chagrin, Marty realizes he did much more than stop a kiss. Without that kiss, none of the other events that led to him and his siblings being born would have happened.

As fate would have it, Marty had a snapshot of himself and his siblings in his jacket pocket. Every time he looked at the snapshot, he would notice his siblings slowly disappearing. Doc explained that they would all disappear if the right set of events weren't set into motion. As every event in the movie unfolded, Marty would look back at the snapshot to see if he was any closer to fixing his mistake and, in essence, existing in the future.

In the speech, the premise of the movie was explained and the speaker then focused on positioning organizations for future success by examining current trends. After every trend was discussed, she reminded the audience members to "look at the snapshot" to see if their organization was one that could expect to survive going into the future. The hook was a hit and was mentioned repeatedly by the audience members after the speech.

Successive Sentences

There are two rhetorical devices that use repetition in successive sentences:

ANAPHORA—the repetition of a word or phrase at the beginning of successive clauses or sentences.

EPISTROPHE—the repetition of a word or phrase at the end of successive clauses or phrases.

In 2008, Barack Obama delivered a concession speech in New Hampshire that changed the face of the Democratic primaries and eventually catapulted him to the presidency. In that speech, he repeated the hook "Yes, we can" 12 times. That hook turned into T-shirts, bumper stickers, mugs...and the rallying cry for his campaign.

I want you to look closely and notice that he used both anaphora and epistrophe.

> We've been asked to pause for a reality check. We've been warned against offering the people of this nation false hope. But in the unlikely story that is America, there has never been anything false about hope.
>
> For when we have faced down impossible odds, when we've been told we're not ready or that we shouldn't try or that we can't, generations of Americans have responded with a simple creed that sums up the spirit of a people: Yes, we can. Yes, we can. Yes, we can. It was a creed written into the founding documents that declared the destiny of a nation: Yes, we can.

It was whispered by slaves and abolitionists as they blazed a trail towards freedom through the darkest of nights: Yes, we can.

It was sung by immigrants as they struck out from distant shores and pioneers who pushed westward against an unforgiving wilderness:
Yes, we can.

It was the call of workers who organized, women who reached for the ballot, a president who chose the moon as our new frontier, and a king who took us to the mountaintop and pointed the way to the promised land: Yes, we can, to justice and equality.

Yes, we can, to opportunity and prosperity. Yes, we can heal this nation. Yes, we can repair this world. Yes, we can.

And so, tomorrow, as we take the campaign south and west, as we learn that the struggles of the textile workers in Spartanburg are not so different than the plight of the dishwasher in Las Vegas, that the hopes of the little girl who goes to the crumbling school in Dillon are the same as the dreams of the boy who learns on the streets of L.A., we will remember that there is something happening in America, that we are not as divided as our politics suggest, that we are one people, we are one nation.

And, together, we will begin the next great chapter in the American story, with three words that

will ring from coast to coast, from sea to shining
sea: Yes, we can.

Whether it's sprinkled throughout your speech or delivered in rapid succession, a hook that's repeated multiple times is likely to catch the ear of the listener.

5. EMOTIONALLY CHARGED WORDS AND PHRASES

Words have the ability to reach down into your soul and touch you on the deepest levels.

Some cut...others heal.

Some bring pleasure...others bring pain.

Some make you optimistic...others make you pessimistic.

But when those words are spoken, they don't just stay in our minds...they live in our hearts. This is one of the reasons we still remember the hook:

"Read my lips: no new taxes!"

Do you ever tell people to read your lips when you're having a pleasant conversation? I don't. If I'm telling someone to read my lips, it's because that person didn't understand what I meant the first, second, or *third* time I said it. If I get to the point of saying "read my lips," it's the last straw!

So when George Bush spoke those words, America took notice. It was the sound bite that was played most often on television and on the radio. It was the phrase that was repeated most often when people discussed the speech. And it was the ammunition that was used against him when he wasn't able to keep his promise.

I know you know I was going to say this again, so here goes... when you combine rhetorical devices, your chances of creating a successful hook increase.

The last device covered was repetition. When you combine emotionally charged phrases with repetition, your chances of creating a hook that catches the ear of your listener increases substantially. "I have a dream" and "Yes, we can" are perfect examples of emotional phrases that were repeated. Every time the phrases were repeated, the level of emotion increased. Whenever you become emotionally involved in what's being said, it's more likely to stay with you.

John Medina, author of *Brain Rules,* makes the case for using emotion in his book. He writes:

> Emotionally charged events are better remembered—
> for longer, and with more accuracy—than neutral
> events. While this idea may seem intuitively obvious,
> it's frustrating to demonstrate scientifically because
> the research community is still debating exactly
> what an emotion is. What we can say for sure is
> that when your brain detects an emotionally charged
> event, your amygdala (a part of your brain that helps
> create and maintain emotions) releases the chemical
> dopamine into your system. Dopamine greatly aids
> memory and information processing. You can think
> of it like a Post-it note that reads "Remember this!"
> Getting one's brain to put a chemical Post-it note on

a given piece of information means that information is going to be more robustly processed. It is what every teacher, parent, and ad executive wants.

6. RHYMES

Rhymes aren't just for children. They're fantastic for creating hooks, too.

The O. J. Simpson trial lasted more than eight months and was covered by all the major news networks. What was the most popular phrase in the whole trial?

"If the glove doesn't fit, you must acquit."

Instant hook.

I don't go out of my way to use poetry in my speeches. That being said, you don't have to be a master at creating rhyming schemes. Google "songwriter's rhyming dictionary" and you'll have a plethora of possible rhymes at your fingertips.

If you want to combine rhyming with another device, I would suggest repetition that's sprinkled throughout your speech. If you repeat a rhyme in rapid succession, it could result in two undesired results:

- A tongue-twister for the speaker.
- An irritated audience. The line "If the glove doesn't fit, you must acquit" wouldn't have had the same level of impact if Johnny Cochrane had repeated it in the style of Dr. King. Just

because a little of something is good, it doesn't necessarily mean a lot will be better.

That being said, the only real way to know how much is enough or too much is to experiment. That's true of both music and speeches.

The possibilities for creating hooks are plentiful. Let's do a quick recap of the six methods that generate the best results:

- Antithesis
- Alliteration
- Lists of three
- Repetition
- Successive sentences
- Emotionally charged words and phrases.
- Rhymes

When you use one, or a combination, of these devices in your speech, the audience will be more likely to remember your speech and repeat your speech to others.

EXERCISES

Choose three of the six rhetorical devices discussed in this chapter you feel most comfortable using. Or feel free to experiment with a rhetorical device you haven't tried before but would like to gain more experience with.

Device 1:

_____

_____

_____

_____

Device 2:

_____

_____

_____

Device 3:

_____

_____

_____

Using the rhetorical devices you chose above, work through some possible hooks for your speech. Remember to read them out loud so you know how they sound to the ear.

So far, we've covered the first two elements of music that are present in successful speeches:

- Chorus
- Hook

In the next chapter, we'll discuss Essential Element #3, the Verses.

ESSENTIAL ELEMENT 3:
THE VERSES

In music, some choruses don't make sense no matter how often you listen to them. That's why verses exist—to explain the story behind the chorus. Even a chorus that makes complete sense can become clearer when verses explain and reinforce the message.

In a speech, you want to have verses that will do the exact same thing: clarify the chorus, tell the story behind the chorus, validate the claims made in the chorus, and add irrefutable evidence to the chorus.

Because even when your chorus is clear and your listeners understand your point of view, they still need to understand *why* you have that point of view.

When you examine popular music, you'll notice all songs are not structured in the same way. Some songs begin with the chorus and then move to the verse. Some songs begin with the verse and then head into the chorus. And there are some songs that don't get to the chorus until late into the song.

In order to make your speech sound like music to their ears, you'll want to vary the verses so you strike the right chord with the audience. Your verses will come in the form of

- metaphors
- analogies
- similes
- stories
- quotations
- statistics

In this chapter, I'm going to give you a brief overview of each item listed. I'll then provide you with a few tips to help you strike the right chord and avoid hitting a sour note.

METAPHORS
— noun (pl.)
The dictionary defines a metaphor as

> "A figure of speech in which a word or phrase that ordinarily designates one thing is used to designate another, thus making an implicit comparison."

If you're anything like me, you'll have to read the above definition a few times before it makes sense. So here's a metaphor to define a metaphor:

"To use a metaphor is to paint word pictures on the canvas of your listeners' minds."

I realize both of those definitions may still have you a little confused, so I'll just list of a few metaphors to make the picture clearer.

An example of a popular metaphor comes from Shakespeare's play, *As You Like It*:

> All the world's a stage,
> And all the men and women merely players:
> They have their exits and their entrances;
> And one man in his time plays many parts,
> His acts being seven ages.

A shorter example of a metaphor is:

> "A mighty fortress is our God."

In both examples, you are saying that one thing *is* another. The world *is* a stage. God *is* a mighty fortress.

More common uses of metaphors in daily language are

> "That news is music to my ears."
> "She has a heart of stone."
> "Life is a journey."

In each instance, the metaphors paint a picture by making an implicit comparison.

How to Use a Metaphor

A metaphor works best when you are trying to create a concrete visual of something that is abstract. Negativity, for example, is an abstract "energy" that exists in organizations, families, and individuals. If you wanted to paint a picture of negativity, you could describe it as a cancer. You could go one step further and use an *extended metaphor* to describe the effects of negativity by saying:

"It eats away at and destroys the places it occupies."

The next time you're tempted to create a visual aid to show a picture, ask yourself how you would describe the picture with words. And you don't need 1,000 words. If you look at the metaphors I've listed, the longest one was 34 words...and it was an *extended* metaphor! All the others are shorter than 20 words.

We think in pictures. When you use metaphors effectively, you are able to create powerful pictures that drive your points home.

ANALOGIES

— noun (pl.)

1. a similarity between like features of two things, on which a comparison may be based: the analogy between the heart and a pump.

2. a form of reasoning in which one thing is inferred to be similar to another thing in a certain respect, on the basis of the known similarity between the things in other respects.

During her keynote address at the 1988 Democratic National Convention, Governor Ann Richards used an effective analogy:

> This Republican Administration treats us as if we were pieces of a puzzle that can't fit together. They've tried to put us into compartments and separate us from each other.

It's easy to confuse metaphors and analogies. The difference between them is slight. The metaphor says one thing *is* another, but an analogy says one thing is *like* the other. Quite frankly, the audience won't care which one you use so long as you use it effectively. I can almost guarantee audience members won't be looking at each other asking, "Was that a metaphor or an analogy?"

How to Use an Analogy

An analogy works well when explaining unfamiliar concepts. When you relate new concepts to something the audience is already familiar with, the learning process is accelerated.

Using an analogy is also powerful when broaching sensitive topics the audience is likely to get defensive about. If you're able to paint a picture or describe a process everyone is familiar with and then clearly link it to the point you want to make, you get past many barriers that can't be broken down with facts alone.

In March 1925 (yes, I've gone a way back to get this example), Margaret Sanger delivered a speech "The Children's Era." In it, she used a vivid analogy of what would be required to make the world a garden for children:

Before you can cultivate a garden, you must know something about gardening. You have got to give your seeds a proper soil in which to grow. You have got to give them sunlight and fresh air. You have got to give them space and the opportunity (if they are to lift their flowers to the sun), to strike their roots deep into that soil. And always—do not forget this—you have got to fight weeds. You cannot have a garden if you let weeds overrun it. So, if we want to make this world a garden for children, we must first of all learn the lesson of the gardener.

SIMILES

— **noun (pl.)**

    1.   a figure of speech in which two unlike things are explicitly compared, as in "she is like a rose."

Both the simile and analogy use "like" or "as" to compare two things. The difference in the comparisons is that the analogy compares two similar things, while the simile compares two things that aren't remotely similar.

> Her kiss is like a cool breeze on a hot sunny day...and
> He's built like a house…

qualify as similes. Unlike the analogy, the simile paints word pictures using little explanation.

How to Use a Simile

Within your speech, similes can be used to inject humorous one liners or insightful motivational nuggets. They can also break up "heavy" sections of a speech. That being said, you need to know your audience well enough to ensure everyone can relate to the comparisons you make.

One of my favorite (and most challenging) speaking experiences happened on the isle of Cyprus. I delivered a session for an international organization whose salespeople came from all over the world for a week-long conference. Many of the participants spoke a minimum of three languages. There were even a few who spoke as many six languages! English was one of those languages, but it was, at best, the third language for anyone hailing from outside the U.S., Canada, or the United Kingdom.

It was my first time presenting to such a diverse audience and I hadn't done my due diligence in researching terms and concepts everyone would be able to relate to. As a result, there were times I used English expressions that were responded to by the simultaneous tilting of heads. Apparently, tilting your head when a speaker says something you don't understand is a universal response. Whenever I saw the heads tilt, I took the signal, paused, and rephrased what I had said.

But even when your audience speaks the same language, it's still important to make sure your references make sense to that audience.

Countries like Canada and the U.S., which share the same borders, will use different words to describe the same thing. I was shocked to find out that a "skipping" rope (Canadian term) is called a "jump" rope in the U.S.

Similarly, different regions in the same country will use different words to describe the same thing. For example, "pop" is also called "soda" in different states.

Do your research to make sure you're not staring into a sea of confused faces and tilted heads when you throw in the occasional simile.

STORIES

—noun (pl.)

1. an account of imaginary or real people and events told for entertainment.
2. an account of past events in someone's life or in the evolution of something.

Since the job of verses in music is to tell the story of the chorus, it stands to reason that stories can be used as verses in speeches. Notice I said "can," not "must."

Despite what you'll hear from many experts, you don't have to use stories to connect with your audience. In fact, if you read through the entire "I Have a Dream" speech, you'll notice stories are nowhere to be found. There are analogies, metaphors, similes and anecdotes, but no stories.

With that being said, Dr. King could probably have read the telephone book and kept you on the edge of your seat. If you're not quite at his level when it comes to keeping the attention of your audience, stories provide you with a reliable vehicle to keep your audience engaged even if you don't have soaring oratory skills.

As with any other "verse," your stories must be relevant. I'm amazed at how many times I've listened to speakers telling stories and thought to myself, *Is there a point to this?* I'm sure you've been there, too. Many presenters make the mistake of using story after story after story, but don't make sure their stories provide substance or clarity to the chorus. When you tell a story, have a point...and make sure the audience clearly understands what that point is.

More about that later...

There are many ways to tell a story. That being said, pay careful attention to the plot of most books and movies and you'll find they all follow a similar pattern. The characters, settings, and challenges will be different, but the pattern remains the same. When you understand the pattern—the winning formula—you're guaranteed success if you follow it. Here's one template you can start with:

- An introduction of the character. It could be a person or an organization.
- A description of the character's day-to-day activities and/or circumstances.
- An unexpected, life-altering event takes place.
- The changes the character makes as a result of the unexpected event.
- The consequences experienced by the character because of the changes the character makes because of the unexpected event.
- The new day-to-day activities and circumstances that result from the changes.

Here's how that would look if I told the story about how I ended up performing in the original cast of the Toronto production of *The Lion King*.

In 1999, John Watkis was an author and professional speaker who traveled the world doing keynote speeches and workshops.

He spent a lot of time in airports, on planes, and going from hotel to hotel.

One day, when John was on a flight home from a business trip, he saw an ad in the paper that read "Singers wanted for *The Lion King*." Besides being a theater arts major in high school, John did a mean karaoke, so he decided to audition.

To his surprise, John was chosen to be the understudy for Mufasa in the original Toronto cast. He became the first Canadian-born actor to play the role.

After a full year of performing eight shows every week, John returned to his first love, professional speaking.

Today, he shares his experiences with audiences in a keynote speech titled "Lessons in the Circle of Life."

As you become more comfortable using this template, you can start adding in the emotions the character felt during the story. That's where the real magic happens.

Once you've crafted your story and put all the pieces in place, there's one more thing you need to do to make the story a success...

You have to tell people the moral of the story.

If you don't, they'll make up one of their own, and it might not be the one you intended.

Everyone interprets information differently. It's been proven that even identical twins watching the same show in the same room don't

ESSENTIAL ELEMENT #3: THE VERSES

see things the exact same way. If you have a room with people from different backgrounds and with different experiences, they're not all going to draw the same conclusion from your story. So make sure to explain the lesson/motive/moral of the story to bring everyone to the same place of understanding.

You can dig deeper and get more information on storytelling from a lot of places. Here are a few I recommend:

The Hero's Journey. It is Christopher Vogler's concise summary of Joseph Cambell's book, *The Hero with a Thousand Faces.* I suggest you read both.

The Story Formula: Mastering the art of connection and engagement through the power of strategic storytelling, by Kelly Swanson. This book walks you, step by step, through the development of stories that help you connect with your audience.

Purposeful Storytelling™ by Michel Neray. This workshop was born from his experience with Mo Mondays, a monthly show of personal storytelling that he founded in Toronto, which has expanded to 14 cities throughout North America. You can find information on his workshops by visiting http://www.neray.com/keynotes

STATISTICS

—noun (pl.)

1. a branch of mathematics dealing with the collection, analysis, interpretation, and presentation of masses of numerical data.
2. a collection of quantitative data.

Yawn!

Sorry if that "yawn" offends you, but numbers and data bore me. As a fan of language and the written word, numbers and I haven't had a harmonious relationship since the 10th grade. I have learned, however, that many people who sit in my audience (and who will be sitting in yours, too) absolutely love data, graphs, charts, and the like. More often than not, these people want you to skip the anecdotal evidence and simply tell them what the numbers say. For them, you can tell all the stories you want, but they'll only be swayed by numerical evidence.

With that in mind, data can be a powerful verse used to give clarity to your chorus. There are, however, pitfalls you'll want to steer clear of. If you simply do a data dump and throw out numbers ad nauseam, you'll leave your audience members shell-shocked, with their eyes scrolling up in their head like slot machines in a Las Vegas casino.

The key to using numbers and data effectively is the same as it is with storytelling...tell your audience members what the numbers *mean*. If you don't, they'll either come to their own conclusions or ignore the information altogether.

Let me tell you a story that illustrates how numbers can leave your audience guessing:

There I was with the toughest crowd anyone could ever do a presentation in front of...my youngest son's kindergarten class. As you can imagine, the children were filled with energy and itching to roll around on the carpet during my presentation, but I had an ace in the hole. I was talking to them about my experiences when I performed in *The Lion King* musical. Their eyes were wide as they *oooed* and *ahhhhed* with every story I told. Then it happened...

I told them the giraffe that walked across the stage was TWENTY FEET TALL! That drew an incredibly loud *Oooooohhhhhh* from the tots. I was just about to continue with the story when the teacher interrupted me and asked the class:

"Does everyone know how tall 20 feet is?"

They all shook their heads in unison and exclaimed without shame... "Noooooooooo."

"Look up at the ceiling," she said. "That's about 20 feet tall."

"Oooooooohhhhhh," they exclaimed, with a newfound understanding. My numbers sounded fascinating to them, but the students in that kindergarten class couldn't conceptualize 20 feet until they had a reference point. The same is true when you use numbers and data in your speeches. Your audience members need to know how those numbers relate to something in their world.

When executives and politicians start throwing out budgets that contain 10 figures, most people can't get a real grasp on it. Most people have never seen that amount of money in their lifetime!

Instead, it's easier for the audience members to wrap their minds around a large figure when it can be compared to something encountered regularly. For example, many salespeople now describe the monthly cost of their products as being equivalent to a cup of coffee a day. If you're going to use that type of comparison, you'll need to clarify if you're speaking about Starbucks coffee.

Rather than throwing out a huge number of people who've tried something, believe something, experienced something, etc., break it down to how many people out of 10. The smaller the number, the easier it is to conceptualize. The easier it is to understand the stats, the less time your audience spends trying to figure out what you meant, and more time actually listening to you. People can't do both at the same time.

QUOTATIONS
—noun (pl.)
1. A group of words taken from a text or speech and repeated by someone other than the original author or speaker.

I'll talk more in depth about quotations when we discuss Essential Element #5, Mood, but I want to touch on it here because of the immediate clarity a quotation can bring to your chorus if used correctly.

ESSENTIAL ELEMENT #3:THE VERSES

In layman's terms, a quotation is a really cool, memorable way of repeating something someone else said. It's succinct and sums up a lot of information using few words.

So when you think about clarifying your chorus, look up applicable quotations online. Just be sure you give credit where credit is due and attribute the quotation to the correct person. It's quite common for the wrong source to be given credit for words that don't belong to or weren't first spoken by that person. The reason this happens is because speakers will often use someone else's quote without attributing it to the person who originally said it.

When you use a quote, make sure to attribute it by saying:

"As my wise Uncle Jethro used to say... "

If you don't know who said something, but you're sure you didn't make it up, you can say:

"A wise person once said..."

That way, you make it clear the quote belongs to someone else.

As you can see, you have an abundance of options for verses to tell your story and make your chorus crystal clear. The key to being successful is using the right mix of verses that complement one another and are harmonious.

Let's recap:

The purpose of verses is to clarify the chorus for your listeners. Your verses can be a combination of

- metaphors
- analogies
- similes
- stories
- quotations
- statistics

EXERCISE: USING VERSES

It's that time again. Let's turn theory into practice. Using the same speech you worked on in the previous chapter, think about three verses you can use to clarify your chorus. To make the exercise more effective, select three different types of verses (for example, metaphor, quotation, and story) and write down the verbiage you would use for each.

Verse 1:

_____

_____

_____

Verse 2:

_____

_____

_____

Verse 3:

_____

_____

_____

So far, we've covered the first three elements required to make a speech sound like music:

- Chorus
- Hook
- Verse

In the next chapter, we'll discuss Essential Element #4, the Pre-chorus.

ESSENTIAL ELEMENT 4:
PRE-CHROUS

I *expected this to be* the shortest chapter in the book. After all, the pre-chorus is usually the shortest part of a song. I thought the chapter would mimic its title. That's not the case.

In order for the pre-chorus to be fully appreciated, I realized I had to describe all the activity that happens on either side of it.

Although it's often taken for granted and barely noticed by the listener, the pre-chorus plays a key role in making the music hit home. After a verse is finished, or after the chorus has been sung with great fervor, the pre-chorus gives you a brief moment to absorb what you heard. At the same time, it signals you're moving from one section of a song to another.

That little interruption in the established pattern of music prevents a blurring of the sections and makes it easy to distinguish one section from another.

Your speech *must* have pre-choruses so your audience can clearly follow your train of thought, have time to digest your most important points, and easily see how ideas connect to each other.

When you give a speech, your audience members don't have the luxury of rewinding you if they get lost along the way. If you keep ploughing ahead without stopping, your audience will be in constant catch-up mode.

It's amazing how often presenters attempt to cram two hours of information into a 30-minute speech by using the Rambo approach to public speaking. They fire off point after point as if they were discharging a machine gun with unlimited ammo. Then they wonder why no one asks questions. The audience is shell shocked, that's why!

Remember, your speech is only successful if your audience remembers, repeats, and responds to it. If you roll ahead at full steam without stopping, the only thing your audience will remember is that you had a lot of content! With that in mind, here are some places within your speech you can use a pre-chorus:

- Using lists
- Moving between major sections in the speech
- Stating different points of view

USING LISTS

If you're listing the "top three," "five worst," or anything that follows a numerical sequence, use a pre-chorus to signal you're moving to the next point and to remind them of the points you've covered. For example

"So far, we've covered three of the EIGHT ESSENTIAL ELEMENTS in music and successful speeches.

#1 was a chorus

#2 was a hook

#3 was verses

Now we'll take a look at #4...the pre-chorus."

When you use this little space, you'll be doing two things:

- You'll be reminding the audience members of the points that are usually forgotten when you continue to add content.
- You'll prevent audience members from trying to remember the previous points when they should be listening to what you're saying. Your listeners can't do both.

MOVING BETWEEN MAJOR SECTIONS OF THE SPEECH

In much the same fashion, and for the same reason as you did with lists, you can use pre-choruses in your speeches simply by reminding your listeners of the major points you want them to keep in their brains. For example, you could say,

> We've identified that music and successful speeches have two things in common. The first thing they have in common is the effect they have on the listener. We discovered that music and successful speeches are remembered, repeated, and responded to by the people who hear them.
>
> The second thing music and successful speeches have in common is that they both contain Eight Essential Elements. Let's take a look at those elements now.

While this may seem redundant, I assure you your audiences will appreciate how easy you make it for them to remember where you've been and to see where they're going next.

DIFFERING POINTS OF VIEW

If you're not including viewpoints that differ from your own during your speeches, you're missing out on an opportunity to reach people in your audience who don't see things from your perspective. If you assume everyone in your audience will see things from your point of view simply because you have data, facts, and a persuasive argument, you're in for a rude awakening.

Don't believe me? Please sit back and watch two people with differing political viewpoints try to prove their point to the other person. They simply try to explain why they feel the way they do while completely ignoring or minimizing the opinion of the other person.

Someone listening to the discussion, who has no vested interest in the debate, can see both sides of the argument, because he or she is not emotionally attached to what is being said. But when both sides are trying to prove their point, each side wants to be heard and understood.

When you're giving a speech, you will have people in your audience who see things differently than you do. The more you try to prove your point, the tighter they clutch to their beliefs, because they don't feel understood by you. But when you can express their point of view the way they would express it themselves, it lets them know that you understand them. And once you let them know you understand them, you can strategically add in a pre-chorus that smoothly crosses them over from defending their point to trying to understand yours. It would sound something like this:

> "One school of thought on this subject is..." (explain the topic from the opposing school of thought).

Then you would add your pre-chorus:

> "Another way of looking at the same situation is..." (explain the topic from your point of view).

One of the best examples I've seen of this technique was during Barack Obama's "A New Beginning" speech at Cairo University in Egypt. Pay close attention to the setup and pre-chorus used in this passage. Once you do that, I want you to tell me how the pre-chorus could have been done more effectively.

> I've come here to Cairo to seek a new beginning between the United States and Muslims around the world, one based on mutual interest and mutual respect, and one based upon the truth that America and Islam are not exclusive and need not be in competition. Instead, they overlap and share common principles—principles of justice and progress, tolerance and the dignity of all human beings.
>
> I do so recognizing that change cannot happen overnight. I know there's been a lot of publicity about this speech, but no single speech can eradicate years

of mistrust, nor can I answer in the time that I have this afternoon all the complex questions that brought us to this point. But I am convinced that in order to move forward, we must say openly to each other the things we hold in our hearts and that too often are said only behind closed doors. There must be a sustained effort to listen to each other, to learn from each other, to respect one another, and to seek common ground. As the Holy Qur'an tells us, "Be conscious of God and speak always the truth." That is what I will try to do today—to speak the truth as best I can, humbled by the task before us, and firm in my belief that the interests we share as human beings are far more powerful than the forces that drive us apart.

Now part of this conviction is rooted in my own experience. I'm a Christian, but my father came from a Kenyan family that includes generations of Muslims. As a boy, I spent several years in Indonesia and heard the call of the *azaan* at the break of dawn and at the fall of dusk. As a young man, I worked in Chicago communities where many found dignity and peace in their Muslim faith.

As a student of history, I also know civilization's debt to Islam. It was Islam—at places like Al-Azhar— that carried the light of learning through so many centuries, paving the way for Europe's Renaissance and Enlightenment. It was innovation in Muslim communities—It was innovation in Muslim communities that developed the order of algebra, our magnetic compass and tools of navigation, our mastery of pens and printing, our understanding of how disease spreads and how it can be healed. Islamic culture has given us majestic arches and soaring spires; timeless poetry and cherished music; elegant calligraphy and places of peaceful contemplation. And throughout history, Islam has demonstrated through words and deeds the possibilities of religious tolerance and racial equality.

I also know that Islam has always been a part of America's story. The first nation to recognize my country was Morocco. In signing the Treaty of Tripoli in 1796, our second President, John Adams, wrote, "The United States has in itself no character of enmity against the laws, religion, or tranquility of Muslims." And since our founding, American Muslims have enriched the United States. They have fought in our wars; they have served in our government; they have stood for civil rights; they have started businesses; they have taught at our universities; they've excelled in our sports arenas; they've won Nobel Prizes, built our tallest building, and lit the Olympic Torch. And when the first Muslim American was recently elected to Congress, he took the oath to defend our Constitution using the same Holy Qur'an that one of our

Founding Fathers—Thomas Jefferson—kept in his personal library.

So I have known Islam on three continents before coming to the region where it was first revealed. That experience guides my conviction that partnership between America and Islam must be based on what Islam is, not what it isn't. And I consider it part of my responsibility as President of the United States to fight against negative stereotypes of Islam wherever they appear.

But, that same principle must apply to Muslim perceptions of America. Just as Muslims—Just as Muslims do not fit a crude stereotype, America is not the crude stereotype of a self-interested empire. The United States has been one of the greatest sources of progress that the world has ever known. We were born out of revolution against an empire. We were founded upon the ideal that all are created equal. And we have shed blood and struggled for centuries to give meaning to those words—within our borders and around the world. We are shaped by every culture, drawn from every end of the Earth, and dedicated to a simple concept: E pluribus unum (out of many, one).

Did you see a place in Obama's speech for a more effective pre-chorus? Let's look a little closer. Obama sang the praises of his listeners and recognized a long list of their accomplishments throughout history.

How do you think that made them feel? How would you feel if a speaker made positive remarks about you and your organization at the start of his or her speech? Pretty good, right?

What I would have changed is Obama's use of the word "but." Again, reflect on how you feel when someone says something nice to you and follows it up with the word "but." What immediately happens? You go on the defensive, because you know whatever comes after the word "but" is going to contradict everything that came before it. The word "however" is no better. Hearing both words is akin to the sound of a screeching, scratching record from the 1980s sitcom, *Ally McBeal*.

A smoother transition would have sounded like this:

> "I believe that same principle must apply to Muslim
> perceptions of America."

See how smooth that was? The transition was made without the abrasive "but" word.

Another pre-chorus you can use when you and your audience have differing points of view is:

> "I can see why you would see it that way. Allow me
> to describe what it looks like from my point of view."

The key to creating the pre-chorus at any point of your speech is to have it flow smoothly from one point to the next. Your goal should be to channel music artists Simon & Garfunkel and create a bridge over troubled waters your listeners can easily cross over in their minds.

Let's recap:

The purpose of the pre-chorus in your speech is to create smooth transitions within your speech. The pre-chorus will:

- Make it easier for your audience to follow your train of thought
- Give your audience time to digest your most important points
- Allow your audience to see how ideas within your speech connect to one another

Places to use a pre-chorus in your speech are when you:

- Use lists
- Move between major sections of the speech
- Have a different point of view than your audience

EXERCISE: USING A PRE-CHORUS

So far, you've created your chorus and your hook, and you've developed verses. In this exercise, you're going to create pre-choruses that connect the verses to one another and to the chorus.

Pre-chorus 1:

_____

_____

_____

_____

Pre-chorus 2:

_____

_____

_____

_____

Pre-chorus 3:

_____

_____

_____

Pre-chorus 4:

_____

_____

_____

_____

We're halfway through! We've covered four of the eight Essential Elements to make your speech music to their ears:

- Chorus
- Hook
- Verses
- Pre-chorus

In the next chapter, we'll be covering Essential Element #5, Mood.

ESSENTIAL ELEMENT 5: MOOD

I'm not the betting type, but I'm willing to bet you own a song. I don't mean a song you wrote. I'm talking about a song you've claimed as your own. A song that will cause you to stop in mid-sentence and drift back to the days of your youth.

I'm talking about a song that, when you hear it start to play, makes you take a deep breath and passionately proclaim...

"That's my song."

I won the bet, didn't I?

Have you ever thought about why certain songs are so special to you? It's because of the way the songs make you feel. That feeling may be attached to happy memories, or maybe even a painful time in your life. Whatever the reason for your attachment to your song, your mood inevitably changes as soon as it starts to play. The opening few notes are all that's required.

In the same way that music establishes or changes your mood, a successful speech will also establish or create a mood for the audience. And in the same way mood is established at the start of a musical piece, mood is established in a successful speech right at the outset.

The mood you set will be determined by the nature of your message, the occasion, and the event where you'll be speaking. Will your speech be serious? Light hearted? Urgent? Celebratory? You'll want to make that clear right from the start.

It's quite possible that members of your audience will be in a mood you want to move them out of. For example, they may be fearful about the possibility of a takeover. You may want to set a tone that acknowledges, but serves to ease, those fears.

The type of mood your audience members are in can and will often influence their willingness to accept your message. I have been in a few situations where the audience didn't want to be there. These were "anger management" sessions for people who management thought needed to be "fixed." When those people came into the room, you knew they didn't want to be there. If I didn't acknowledge their mood in the beginning of my talk, it would have been an uphill struggle. But because I did acknowledge where they were emotionally, many, though not all, were far more willing to engage in the sessions.

Let me give you an example of how I started with people who were attending sessions on anger management or how to deal with conflict in the workplace. Because I knew they didn't necessarily want to be there, I would start by saying something I didn't make up, but heard one day when I was taking a college course. It met me where I was at the time, so I "borrowed" it and tweaked it to fit my delivery style.

I would say to them:

> *Listen, I know in this room, there are three different groups of people. The first group of people, they're what I call learners. And when you heard that we were doing a session on conflict management, you were happy. You thought, If I can get one or two pieces of information that will help me to handle my conflict a little more effectively, it'll be a good day. So if you're a learner and you're here today, I promise you'll get one or two pieces of information that you didn't know before.*

Then I would say:

> *If you're not a learner, then you might fit into the second group of people who are here, and they're what I call vacationers. And if you're a vacationer, you're just happy to have the day off.*

That usually gets a laugh, because people identify with a "paid vacation." And then I say to them:

> *Well, if you're a vacationer, have you ever been on vacation and found out one or two things about the*

destination you were at that you didn't know about before?

I get people nodding their heads and then I say:

Great! As you're here today, I want you to enjoy your-self. I want you to enjoy your vacation, but I still want you to walk away with one or two ideas that will help you to manage your conflict.

I would follow that with:

If you're not a learner, and you're not a vacationer, that puts you into the third group of people. You're what I call prisoners...and you feel like you've been sentenced here today.

Right at that moment, I get a lot of heads nodding and looking at me, and the arms actually start to unfold. Why? Because I've identified where they are emotionally and mentally. And I say:

Well, listen, if you're a prisoner, this is going to be the shortest sentence you could possibly ever have. But since you do have to be here, why not get the best out of it and try and walk away with one or two points so that the people who are really at fault—you know, the other people—will not get to you as much when you go back to work. And hopefully by the end of the day, you'll leave here being, at least, a vacationer having enjoyed yourself.

All I'm doing is acknowledging where they are emotionally and how they're feeling about the session...and I do it right at the beginning. Because if I just started out happy as punch, many of them would glare at me to let me know "I don't want to be here and there's nothing you're going to do or say that's going to make me happy to be here."

Depending on the event activities, it's quite possible your audience may not be physically able to digest a dynamic opening if you deliver the first remarks of the day. In my early years as a presenter, I did sessions over a couple of days at a conference in Kingston, Ontario, Canada. The event organizer was kind enough to let me know I would be presenting the morning following the company party. At the time, it meant nothing to me, but I understood her reason for providing that detail when I came face to face with a number of hungover participants who did well to make it out of their rooms that morning.

Can you imagine the impact of a loud, attention-grabbing opening for that group? Had I asked everyone to stand up and do something interactive right off the bat, it could have been a messy situation. I've since learned to ask what activities will be taking place prior to me speaking.

Once you've figured out the mood your audience members will be in and the mood you want them to be in, there are a variety of ways you can begin your speech.

"THANK YOU"

Despite claims to the contrary, audience members will not automatically tune you out if you begin by thanking them for attending. They won't be offended. They won't collect all their belongings and make a beeline to the exit. Thanking the people in attendance is polite. After all, they've taken time out of their day to listen to you and they've taken the time to be there. Thanking the person who introduced you is polite. Thanking the person who invited you to speak is polite. It doesn't take a tremendous amount of time to say the words, and it does help break the ice with your audience. Especially if the audience has never heard of you, they'll need a little time to adjust to the sound of your voice. While you're thanking everyone to start off with, you're also giving the audience an opportunity to move their focus from whatever they were doing to what you want them to do. I'll admit it's neither captivating nor shocking, but that's not why you say "thank you." You say it because you're genuinely appreciative of the people attending and listening.

Also, if you think about it, if you have people who are chatting with one another in a large conference meeting, they may be in the midst of their conversation. And if you start off and try and grab their attention immediately, they may miss what you say at the beginning. That "thank you" gives them that opportunity to make the transition over to you and to give you their attention.

MAKE REFERENCE TO THE CITY, VENUE, DATE, OR THEME OF A MEETING

Very often, there are interesting and relevant tidbits of information about the city, venue, or date of your speech that can serve as the perfect opening statements and help segue smoothly into your topic.

Martin Luther King, Jr. did this in his "I Have a Dream" speech when he said:

> *Five score years ago, a great American, in whose symbolic shadow we stand, signed the emancipation proclamation.*

Of course, King was referring to the statue of Abraham Lincoln which stands in the Lincoln Memorial. In referring to the statue of Lincoln, King was also providing himself with ammunition for what else he was about to say. Think of it...he had "Abe" to back him up.

In his speech at the 2004 Republican convention in New York, Rudolph Giulianni's opening remarks were perfect for the occasion and the location. Keep in mind what had happened in New York three years prior. Planes crashed into the Twin Towers and killed hundreds of unsuspecting, innocent victims. Also, keep in mind the outpouring of love the city had been receiving from people all over the world.

Look at how he wove the history of New York into his speech. Giulliani started by saying:

> *Welcome to the capital of the world...New York.*

This drew a great applause from the audience. He then went on to say:

> *New York was the first capital of our great nation. It was here in 1789 in lower Manhattan that George Washington took the oath of office as the first President*

of the United States. And it was here in 2001 in the same lower Manhattan that President George W. Bush stood amid the fallen towers of the World Trade Center, and he said to the barbaric terrorists who attacked us, "They will hear from us."

After a few statements about the accomplishments of President Bush, Giulliani went back to his New York references.

This is the first Republican convention ever held here in New York City. In fact, I've never seen so many Republicans in New York City. It's great! Great! I finally feel at home!

And you know something? Mayor Blumberg, Governor Pataki—all of you that worked so hard in bringing this convention to New York—our President, and the Party that decided to have it here, above everything else it's a statement. It's a strong statement that New York City and America are open for business, and we are stronger than ever!

Of course, Giulliani was speaking on behalf of George W. Bush, but he front-loaded his remarks, created momentum, and developed a connection with the audience by referencing New York first. So you can see how researching the city can have a great impact on the opening of your speech.

I used this method when I spoke to over a hundred young leaders from sub-Saharan Africa at a conference in Washington, D.C. I had traveled to D.C. for the event and tied in relevant points about the city to the topic "The Art of Public Speaking":

> Whenever I visit Washington, D.C., I make a point of visiting the Lincoln Memorial. I walk up the long set of stairs and search for the spot where Dr. Martin Luther King Jr. stood when he delivered the "I Have a Dream" speech. I look out over the presidential lawn and imagine how it must have felt to deliver the speech to such an enormous crowd.
>
> When Dr. King delivered that speech, he wasn't as popular as he is today. In fact, he had to be courageous to deliver a message he knew wouldn't be popular with most people. He was only in his early 30s at the time...not much older than you.
>
> Despite the resistance he faced, Dr. King spoke those words because he knew he had a chance to change the circumstances many faced by standing up and speaking out. Dr. King once said, "In the end, we will remember not the words of our enemies, but the silence of our friends."
>
> The next hour we spend together is not just about tips and tools to make you better public speakers. It's about equipping you to speak on behalf of those who cannot speak for themselves and who will continue to suffer if you choose to remain silent.

If the speech is being held on a significant day in history, or if there's a holiday or event that fits into the context of your speech, you may want to incorporate it into your speech. Keep in mind that many events are held just to celebrate specific days and people. Google "this day in history," and you'll have all the information you need at your fingertips.

If you're speaking at a conference, you can also use the theme of the event as a place to start. Make a comment about the appropriateness of the theme, how it fits into your daily life, or why you think it's such a timely message.

I did this when I spoke at a "Staff Day" celebration for a group of nearly 700 employees. The theme for the day was "The Magic in Us." To start off the day, a magician made the department head magically appear. To tie my opening into the theme, I made reference to the trick that had taken place that morning.

> *I understand you had a magician make Dr. Mowat appear this morning. I didn't share this with the event organizers, but I've been working on a few magic tricks myself. So for my first trick of the afternoon, I'm going to make Dr. Mowat disappear!*

As I expected, that drew a few laughs.

> *Just kidding. I couldn't do a magic trick to save my life. But that's not to say that my life hasn't been a little bit of a miracle.*

I then went on to introduce myself to the audience and tie in the theme of "The Magic in Us" to "potential."

COMMON TRAITS BETWEEN THE SPEAKER AND THE AUDIENCE.

If you are not an industry expert, some audience members will feel as if you don't fully understand their challenges or day-to-day operations. If your occupation is different than that of your audience members, they may not think you're credible to address them on certain issues. If your audience knows you have a different point of view on a sensitive issue, its members most likely will be resistant from the very start. If you are proficient at doing certain tasks and someone is just trying to learn those tasks, that person may forget you had to struggle through the learning stages as well. In all of the aforementioned situations, it would be a good idea to establish the similarities that exist between you and your audience:

- Identify where you share common challenges.
- Point out how your views are more similar than different.
- List experiences you've had with other audiences or clients who are similar to the people you're speaking to that day.
- Talk about the frustrations you've had with the issue you're about to discuss.

ESTABLISH YOUR CREDIBILITY...TELL YOUR STORY

If the background information of your topic is interesting or unique, share it with the audience members. It's an effective way to convince them you're the most credible person to be speaking on that particular topic. Have you done research no one else has done? Have you interviewed experts and summarized the results? Have you been part of a special movement? Does your organization use processes no other organization uses? Have you received an award? Overcome a commonly faced challenge? There are times when sharing this information will make your audiences lean forward in their seats to hear what you have to say.

In his book *8 to be Great,* originally published in 2007, Richard St. John shares a story about sitting beside a little girl in an airplane when she asked him about how to become successful. He didn't have the answer then, but he decided he wanted to find out. In 10 years of studies, he interviewed over 500 successful people, including Bill Gates, Steve Jobs, and Russell Crowe. Even if Richard St. John hadn't been a successful businessperson, his interviews with such a large number of successful people would still have provided him with the credibility to speak about success. Why? Because he tells his story. And if there is something unique about the way you gathered the information you're going to share with the audience members, telling your story is a good idea, too.

As much as I love standing in front of a crowd and speaking, I was equally as cautious about sharing my performance stories with my audiences. I felt I would take away from the focus of the subject if I brought up points about my background I didn't deem relevant to my teaching points. I know I was not alone in feeling this way, because I have since coached many clients out of this mindset.

The greatest shift I had around telling my story occurred in front of an unlikely audience. The audience was made up of incarcerated youths who had committed serious crimes. My contact at the prison pointed out this was not a group of repentant fellows. They were repeat offenders and expected to make the transition to the adult system once they were of age.

During my first presentation to the group, we got off to a rocky start. I came across as hard core and gave them my best "tough love" talk. I didn't quite get the reaction I was hoping for. Then something happened. I asked the young men to tell me about something they were good at and liked to do. One by one, they shared examples of what they were good at and areas they were gifted in. The guards were all stunned. They told me they were learning things about the inmates they had never heard before.

As the young men began to open up and share their gifts, I told them about my time performing in *The Lion King*. Before I knew it, they were asking me to sing and do the voice of "Mufasa" for them. When I shared my story, the connection was instantaneous.

The next time I went to speak at the youth prison, I changed my opening. I began with the shout from *The Lion King* and shared my story with them. We had an instant connection and the young men were immediately open to hearing what I had to say.

You may not have performed in a famous musical, but it's not something you need to have done in order for your story to be relevant to your audience. When you share your story as it relates to the topic at hand, you'll create a connection with your listeners that will make them want to hear what you have to say.

START WITH A STATISTIC

Starting with a "shocking statistic" is a favorite technique of many presenters. For the record, the statistic doesn't need to be shocking or startling. All it needs to do is give your audience members information that will gain their attention and or advance their understanding of your topic. If you succeed in shocking them, great...but don't feel you need to. What you will want to do is present the statistic in a way that is relevant and easy for the audience to understand (see Essential Element #3, the Verses).

START WITH A STORY

Everyone loves a story. Well...almost everyone. Stories are probably the safest way to start a speech, but only if they're told correctly. You aren't entitled to tell the same type of story to begin your speech as you are in the middle of your speech. Both types of stories should be relevant and lead to a purpose within your speech, but the story to start a speech should be shorter and more to the point. If your first story drags on too long, people will become impatient. Even if you're a celebrity, people will want to know where this is all going.

SONG

As with stories, everyone loves music. There's a good chance that there's a song which will serve as a great opening. For example, in my speech called "The Magic in Us," I begin with "Magic," by Olivia Newton-John. When I do my talk on "How to Make Your Speech Sound Like Music to Their Ears," I begin by playing "Just Like Music," by Eric Sermon and Marvin Gaye. This works best in a convention setting with large audiences. If you do use music to open your speech, be sure to investigate the legalities behind it.

In Canada, contact SOCAN. In the United States, contact ASCAP or BMI.

If you're outside of North America, you'll want to Google "music creators and publishers" within your country to get accurate information.

You may not think it's a big deal, but it's better to be safe than sorry. By the same token, it's also the right thing to do. Musicians should be compensated for their contributions and creativity.

QUOTATIONS/CLICHÉS/SONG LYRICS

Using quotations, clichés, or song lyrics is another safe and effective way of starting a speech. This technique can capture the attention of the audience, provide you with an authoritative point of view, and set the tone for the speech. There are two ways you can use a quotation to open your talk.

The first way is to use the quote and explain why it's true. The second way—and the one I prefer to use—is to use a quote or cliche and question the validity of it. By questioning a famous quote or commonly accepted cliché, you're provoking your audience to think. It's an unexpected and attention-grabbing method. Questioning a quote or cliché also sets you up as an independent thinker who has something different to say. I used this method when I wrote a speech for a client on the topic of networking:

> There's an old saying everyone has heard...and probably said at some point in his or her life. The saying sums up, for many people, the secret to success in business and life in general: "It's not what you know, it's who you know."
>
> But is that true?

Does your success, does your ability to get promoted at work, to land your dream job, to have your proposals accepted—Does it really come down to who you know? Not what you know?

I would have to say, yes...but there's more to it.

It's not just about what you know or who you know. It's about the perception that other people have of you. You may know a lot of people, but that won't do you any good unless those people like you, trust you, and think you're competent.

Because if they like you, trust you, and think you're competent, they'll be more likely to give you business. They'll be more likely to consider you for a job opening. They'll be more likely to hear you out when you have a proposal. When they like you, trust you, and think you're competent, success, no matter how you define it, becomes more attainable.

But if you want people to like you, trust you, and think you're competent, you'll have to avoid the major mistakes that people make when they're networking. That's what I'll be sharing with you over the next few minutes. How to avoid the major mistakes that networkers make so you can be more successful in business and everyday life.

The next time you think about starting your speech with a quote or cliché, try to put a spin on it that will get your audience thinking.

STARTING WITH A QUESTION

When you ask your audience members a question, you're engaging them and drawing them in to whatever you're speaking about. There are a variety of ways to make questions work for you.

The Rhetorical Question

"Why are we here today?" is a common question I've heard many executives use to begin their speeches. Sometimes the audience answers out loud, other times they'll answer in their heads or whisper a snide remark to the person beside them. Either way, asking the question automatically gets some form of response from the audience.

The Multiple-Choice Question

If you really want to draw your audience in...and if the situation allows for it, use the multiple-choice question. When running presentation skills seminars, I have participants come to the front and practice their speeches. During one of my sessions, a participant used the multiple-choice question technique to begin her speech. The first question was an audience participation question...

"Does anyone in the audience know what aphasia is?"

Most of the audience gave her blank stares, but one person knew it was a "lack of something." The presenter went on to explain that aphasia was a lack of language. Once the audience members knew the answer to the question, they all gave a collective *Ohhh* to signal their understanding. But rather than simply giving her listeners the statistics on aphasia (which would have been fine), she engaged them again by asking another question.

> *"Does anyone want to guess how many people in Canada have aphasia?"*

Once again, she had the audience thinking. That's when she used the multiple-choice technique.

> *"Would you say it's 100? 1,000? How about 5,000? Would you believe..."*

The presenter went on to give the stats and segue into her main points. She could have simply given the stats without asking questions of the audience, but by asking the questions, she drew people in, created anticipation, and piqued their curiosity. The next time you prepare a speech, look for ways to ask a question that will engage the audience and draw its members into your speech.

JOKES

The advice on starting with a joke is confusing. Some people tell you to always start with a joke. Others will tell you never start with a joke. Depending on whom you ask, starting with a joke is either the best strategy or the worst strategy. I agree with both points of view.

Humor is said to be the shortest distance between two people, so it's easy to see why you would want to get your audience laughing right off the bat. If your joke succeeds, you have instant rapport with your audience. On the other hand, a joke can completely put you at odds with your audience if it's told poorly, is in bad taste, or has absolutely nothing to do with the speech you're about to give. So I wouldn't say you should always start with a joke, but I wouldn't say you should never start with a joke either. What would I say? I would say the same thing I say about the best way to start a speech: "It depends."

There are two important factors to take into consideration. The first factor has to do with the appropriateness of the joke. Even though the joke may be funny, it may be inappropriate because of the speaker, the audience, or the occasion. For example, a younger person telling a joke about senior citizens to a group of senior citizens might be seen as offensive or disrespectful. On the other hand, a senior citizen telling the same joke could get away with it.

U.S. Senator John McCain was widely criticized for his "Bomb Iran" joke he told during the 2008 presidential election, but the audience he told it to actually laughed. If you watch the video, you'll see the response he gets from the audience is quite positive. Unfortunately for McCain, his real audience was much bigger than the people who were seated in the room that day. EVERYTHING is captured on video these days, so always keep your global audience in mind when you speak.

Religious and political jokes are ones you usually want to stay away from, but on March 8, 1983, President Ronald Reagan began his speech at the 41st Annual Convention for the National Association of Evangelicals with a joke about a politician and clergyman. After thanking the group for their prayers and support, this is what Reagan said:

From the joy and the good feeling of this conference, I go to a political reception. Now, I don't know why, but that bit of scheduling reminds me of a story which I'll share with you.

An evangelical minister and a politician arrived at heaven's gate one day together. And St. Peter, after doing all the necessary formalities, took them in hand to show them where their quarters would be. And he took them to a small, single room with a bed, a chair, and a table and said this was for the clergyman. And the politician was a little worried about what might be in store for him. And he couldn't believe it then when St. Peter stopped in front of a beautiful mansion with lovely grounds, many servants, and told him that these would be his quarters.

And he couldn't help but ask, he said, "But wait, how—there's something wrong—how do I get this mansion while that good and holy man only gets a single room?" And St. Peter said, "You have to understand how things are up here. We've got thousands and thousands of clergy. You're the first politician who ever made it.

But I don't want to contribute to a stereotype. So I tell you there are a great many God-fearing, dedicated, noble men and women in public life, present company included. And yes, we need your help to keep us ever-mindful of the ideas and the principles that brought us into the public arena in the first place.

From there, Reagan went on to deliver a speech now known as "The Evil Empire."

As you can see, there are times when telling a joke can work. You have to be absolutely sure the joke is appropriate.

I said there are two factors you'll need to consider if you want to start your speech with a joke. The first one being, is it appropriate? The second factor you'll need to consider has to do with the person telling the joke. And it all comes down to one question: Is the person funny? The question is much easier to answer if you're writing the speech for someone else. You know whether or not a person is funny and has the timing it takes to tell a joke. You're also painfully aware if that person might butcher a joke beyond recognition. Unfortunately, everyone thinks he or she is funny. And most people don't know that they're not as funny as they think.

When comedians tell a joke, they make it look easy, but that's because they've practiced hard and have a gift for good timing. When the average person tells the same joke, it doesn't have the same effect. This simple truth is lost on many a presenter. So here's my advice to you if you're writing *and* delivering the speech...show the joke to someone who isn't afraid of you and who you know will give you honest feedback. I'm serious about this. If people are afraid of you or the repercussions that may follow for telling you their true thoughts, they'll most likely tell you exactly what you want to hear. And when the joke falls flat in front of an audience, you'll think to yourself, *Well so-and-so thought it was funny. It's probably just the audience.* More often than not, it's not the fault of the audience at all. Once again, I'm not saying you should never start with a joke, but if you insist on it, make sure you put it under a powerful microscope first.

HUMOR

Even if you're not gifted in the joke-telling department, it's still possible to use humor at the start of your speech. Using humor and telling jokes are not the same. Jokes have a punchline...humor doesn't have to. With jokes, your goal is to get a laugh. With humor, your goal is to get a smile and lighten the mood. I once witnessed a presenter use humor during a session on organizing your life. She asked the participants to stand, and keep standing, if anything she said pertained to them. She proceeded to run off a number of scenarios:

- you have receipts in your wallet for items you can no longer return
- you have keys on your key rings but don't know what door they open
- you have the original picture that came with your wallet
- you have pictures of people that you don't even recognize in your wallet
- you have clothes in your closet that you haven't thrown away because you're waiting for them to come back in style

Anyone asking those questions would have gotten, at the very least, some big smiles from the audience. No joke-telling skills would be required. So if your goal is to "break the ice" or build rapport with your audience, try humor if you're not sure you can pull off telling jokes.

For more information on how to incorporate humor into your speeches and presentations, check out *Speaking of Funny: 77 Ways to Add Humor to Any Presentation,* by David Glickman.

Let's recap:

The role of mood in your speech is to set the appropriate tone from the moment you begin your speech. The mood you set is determined by the audience and the event. Once you determine what mood your audience members will be in and what mood you want them to be in, you can start your speech with

- Thank you
- Make reference to the city/venue/date/theme of the meeting
- Common ground between speaker and audience
- Your story/credentials

- Statistic
- Story
- Song
- Quotation/Cliché/Song Lyrics
- Question
- Joke/Humor

EXERCISE: MOOD

At this point, you should have a speech that contains a chorus, hook, verses, and pre-choruses. Now it's time to set the mood. If you don't have a speech coming up, think of one you've done in the past and use the audience and occasion to determine which of the opening strategies is most appropriate.

Opening Strategy:

_____

_____

_____

_____

Once you've determined what your opening strategy is going to be, write it out in the space below. If you need more space, use a separate sheet of paper.

_____

_____

_____

_____

_____

_____

We're almost there! We've covered five of the eight essential elements to make a speech sound like music to their ears:

- Chorus
- Hook
- Verses
- Pre-chorus
- Mood

In the next chapter, we'll be covering Essential Element #6, Rhythm.

ESSENTIAL ELEMENT 6:
RHYTHM

Finally! I was going to get my chance. I'd been waiting for this opportunity for years and now I was only seconds away from getting my shot.

Two years earlier when Mrs. Pugh selected the fifth graders who would play the steel drums, I was overlooked. It burned me, because I had always loved the sound of the steel drums and imagined myself playing the thunderous, dance-inducing instruments under the guidance of Earl La Pierre, the most recognized local musician in the community. But this time I couldn't be overlooked.

It was seventh grade music class and Mr. Ferguson, the music teacher, made the call for anyone who wanted to play the drums. We were told to stand over in the corner beside the worn-looking drum set we all coveted.

Mr. Ferguson, who we sometimes called "Fergie" or "Fergs" (but never to his face), was a mountain of a man. At the time, I stood 5 feet, 5 inches tall and weighed about 120 pounds soaking wet, so Mr. Ferguson seemed larger than life. He was shaped like the Kool-Aid guy and entered the room with equal energy. When he opened his mouth, it sounded like a symphony. Somehow, he managed to include the soprano, alto, and tenor to his words when he spoke. Most amazing was his ability to play the clarinet, saxophone, tuba, French horn, trumpet, and flute with equal ease. And the drums... he could also play the drums.

Seven of us lined up and listened intently to Mr. Ferguson as he gave instructions on how to play. My eyes stayed locked on him as he positioned himself, wrapped his thick fingers around the drumsticks and proceeded to play the rhythm he wanted us to repeat. "This is where you sit. This is where you place your feet. This is how you hold the drumsticks. This is what I want you to play."

One by one, we each had our moment at the drums and did our best to recreate exactly what Mr. Ferguson had played. I felt laser focused and overcome with awe and joy all at the same time. When I finished, I was sure I had nailed it.

I was wrong.

Before the echo from the last strike, played by the last student, could disappear, Mr. Ferguson announced Mike would be the drummer. I was stunned by how quickly the decision was made, but then Mr. Ferguson clearly explained how he came to his decision. In that same moment, he also taught me a lesson I'll carry with me to my grave...

Seven of us sat down to play the drums, but only one of us held the drumsticks the way Mr. Ferguson had demonstrated. We were all so focused on playing, we ignored the fundamentals and went straight for the fun. This is why I ended up playing the tenor sax.

Everything we covered in this book so far should be considered "how you hold the sticks."

Developing a chorus is "how you hold the sticks."

Creating a catchy hook is "how you hold the sticks."

Using verses is "how you hold the sticks."

Setting the mood is "how you hold the sticks."

Using pre-choruses is "how you hold the sticks."

Essential elements 1 through 5 are all fundamentals you have to have solidified in your speech before you tinker with the fun elements. The first of these fun elements is rhythm.

In the first chapter, I said you didn't have to possess musical talents to benefit from the principles in this book. You don't. It will, however, be helpful for you to understand a little fundamental music theory.

Stay with me! I promise it will be painless if this is your first music theory lesson. If you're already a whiz at music theory, try to predict how I'll be tying in rhythm to your speeches.

Musically inclined or not, I know you understand that rhythm plays a major role in the structure of music. That's why people will tell you they don't have rhythm when someone brings up the prospect of dancing. The truth is, everyone has rhythm. That person may not be able to stay on beat, but he or she does have rhythm.

What's the difference?

In music, a beat is the regular pulse of music. Think of the steady clicking sound of the second hand on a watch, or the sound of a steady heartbeat. A beat is consistent.

Rhythm, on the other hand, is the variation of the duration of sounds (notes) within a certain time frame. I realize the definition requires a double-take, so I've added a table of notes used in music. It will better explain what "variation of the duration of sounds" looks like. Each note is played or sung for a specific amount of time.

Symbol	Name	Value
𝐨	Whole note	Gets four beats
𝅗𝅥	Half note	Gets two beats
♩	Quarter note	Gets one beat
♪	Eighth note	Gets half a beat

The most common time in music is 4/4 time. This means there are four beats in a measure of music (bar).

Using the musical notes listed in the chart, you could use a whole note, two half notes, four quarter notes, or eight eighth notes to get four beats.

You could also use:

One half note and two quarter notes
One half note, one quarter note, and two eighth notes
Four eighth notes and one half note

In all of the combinations I've listed, each adds up to four beats.

ESSENTIAL ELEMENT #6:RHYTHM

The takeaway from this brief exercise is to give you a feel for how you can fill the exact same space of time while varying the length of the notes.

Let's connect it back to your speeches.

Since rhythm in music is the variation of the duration of sounds within a certain time frame, rhythm in a speech would be defined as:

> The variation of word length and sentence structure within phrases.

The key word in all of this is "variation." Mix it up when you're speaking!

I've read well-intentioned, but misguided, advice that you should only speak in sound bites so the media can quote you more easily.

Seriously? Stop it.

Sound bites don't have to be short.

I'm going to ask you to go back and reread the last section (from "I've read well-intentioned..."). I gave you a long sentence with multi-syllabic words and then threw in one-word and two-word sentences. I varied the sentences in two ways:

1. Sentence length
2. Syllable count

This variation in sentence structure is more interesting and provides a better flow than if you simply kept your sentences short or overcomplicated everything and bombarded your audience with big words that required a dictionary to understand.

I'm going to backtrack and address the theory I mentioned above.

Speaking in shorter sentences doesn't automatically qualify as speaking in sound bites. On the flip side, using long sentences doesn't disqualify you from creating sound bites. Think of some of the most oft-quoted sections of speeches that have been replayed and quoted in print for decades. They aren't considered sound bites because of their length. It's because of the impact those words carried. For example

> I have a dream that one day, my four children will live in a nation where they will not be judged by the color of their skin, but by the content of their character.

Not short, right? But it was still a sound bite. It *is* still a sound bite. How about this one?

> Ask not what your country can do for you. Ask what you can do for your country.

Shorter? Yes, but not short.

You want sound bites? Say something significant.

But I digress...

If you take stock of how we speak, you'll notice rhythm is already embedded in our daily conversations. When you tell someone your telephone number, you use the same rhythm every time.

The same thing is true when people give you their phone number and you have to remember it because you don't have a pen. You repeat the number to yourself using the same rhythmic pattern the person used when giving it to you. See? You've got rhythm!

If you're not quite sure how to apply the principle of rhythm to your speeches in a practical way, here's what I suggest:

Write, read out loud, and rewrite

When musicians write songs, they don't put it all on paper and then play the piece. They'll either play it and write it down, or they'll write a section of music and then test it out.

This is how you should test the rhythm of your speeches. Once you've written something down, read it out loud to experience what it sounds like and how it feels to say it. Reading it in your head and saying it out loud will give you two completely different experiences. Go ahead and try it. Read the following sentences in your head, then read them out loud to see if you can feel the difference in both the rhythm and impact.

> These are the times that try men's souls.
> Times like these try the souls of men.

> We cannot dedicate, we cannot consecrate, we cannot hallow this ground.
> We cannot dedicate, consecrate, or hallow this ground.

> This government of the people, by the people, for the people...
> This government of the people, this government by the people, this government for the people...

If you didn't notice a difference in the first example, I'm betting you didn't read it out loud. If that's the case, go back. The sentences feel different coming out of your mouth and will reach the ears of the audience differently.

I also want you to notice that a technique may have worked with one phrase, but when the same technique was used with a different phrase, it didn't have the same effect. This is why you have to write, read out loud, and rewrite.

> The notes I handle no better than many pianists. But the pauses between the notes—*ah,* that is where the art resides.
>
> — *Artur Schnabel*

We've covered a lot of information on the importance of variation in note length, but, as Artur Schnabel points out, your words will be brought to life by the pauses in between. In music, those pauses are referred to as "rests." In speeches, the term most frequently used is "pause."

As is the case with notes, different marks indicate how long each rest will last. The chart below shows the different rests and how many beats are given for each.

Symbol	Name	Value
▀▀	Whole Rest	Gets four beats
▄▄	Half Rest	Gets two beats
𝄽	Quarter Rest	Gets one beat
𝄾	Eighth Rest	Gets half a beat

As you can imagine, each rest is going to create a different effect. The only way to truly discover what the effect will be is to say the words out loud and play with the pauses.

Watch comedians closely and you'll see how important a pause is to the success or failure of a joke. It's rare for a setup line to be immediately followed by a punch line with no pause in between. I'm not saying it doesn't happen. I'm saying it's rare.

Using pauses is effective for more than getting laughs. You can use pauses to

- Give the audience time to laugh
- Clearly signal the end of a thought
- Give the audience time to answer a question
- Allow the audience time to repeat or reflect on a quote or point you made
- Create anticipation for what you're about to say next
- Cause the audience to become squeamish and uncomfortable (yes...on purpose)
- Eliminate "um," "ah," and other fillers from your sentences

- Make eye contact, connect with audience members, and take the temperature of the mood in the room
- Give the audience a chance to formulate questions about what you just said

As you can clearly see from the list, there's power in a pause. But if it's so powerful, why don't we use it more?

Good question.

In my opinion, many speakers simply don't think they have enough time to pause. They feel the need to cram so much content into their allotted time slot that stopping to say nothing seems illogical. If that's your issue with pausing during your speeches, I encourage you to reduce the quantity of your content and beef up the quality. Here's why...differing studies will give you differing percentages on how much of your content your audience will remember after your speech. What doesn't differ in the research is that your audience members will forget far more of your content than they will remember. By an overwhelming amount! In other words, the more content you throw at them in a short period of time, the more they will forget.

On the other hand, if you give less content, more solid examples, and allow time for the audience to reflect on the content you present, there is a far greater likelihood the audience will remember, repeat, and respond to what you say. Remember how to determine if your speech was successful?

Incorporating the variation of word and sentence length with the power of the pause into your speeches is more of an art than a science. You have to be willing to play with your words until they feel right when you say them. And it can't be said enough times... read your speech out loud. That's the only way you'll know if you've got something that strikes the right chord and sounds like music to their ears.

Let's recap:

Rhythm is the variation of word length and sentence structure within phrases. Your phrases can be varied using:

1. Sentence length
2. Syllable count

Using the power of the pause throughout your speech provides multiple benefits to both the audience and the speaker.

EXERCISE: RHYTHM

Choose any passage within the speech you've been preparing and write it in the space below.

_____

_____

_____

_____

Experiment with the same passage by using making your sentences and/or words longer or shorter. _Read them out loud._

_____

_____

_____

_____

Identify areas within your speech where you can purposefully pause. Write down the section of the speech you've chosen and read it out loud while pausing for differing lengths of time. Take note of the different feel your words take on based on the length of your pause.

_____

_____

_____

_____

_____

_____

_____

We've covered the first six of the eight essential elements that make a speech sound like music to their ears:

- Chorus
- Hook
- Verse
- Pre-chorus
- Mood
- Rhythm

In the next chapter, we'll discuss Essential Element #7, Expression.

ESSENTIAL ELEMENT 7: EXPRESSION

There's an old cliché:

It's not what you said, it's how you said it.

This is true in both music and speeches. What you play *and* what you say are both important. I want to be clear about that. But "how" you play a note or say a word will change the entire meaning and/or interpretation of that note or word.

In keeping with the pattern I've established so far, I'll show you how this happens in music, then I'll relate it to giving a speech.

In music, "how" you play a note is referred to as "expression." Wikipedia defines expression as:

The art of playing or singing with a personal response to the music. At a practical level, this means making appropriate use of dynamics, phrasing, timbre, and articulation to bring the music to life.

Britannica.com defines musical expression this way:

> That element of musical performance which is something more than mere notes.

In order to incorporate expression into a piece of music, expression markings are added. Below, I've provided a chart of symbols used in music to add expression along with a brief definition of each. This is not an exhaustive list. It will, however, provide you with enough examples to review and experiment with.

You may be surprised to find you're already familiar with some of the musical expressions. That's because the terminology is used in our daily vocabulary.

Expression Term	Symbol	Definition
Crescendo	$<$	Gradually get louder
Decrescendo/ Diminuendo	$>$	Gradually get softer
Forte	*f*	Perform loudly
Piano	*p*	Perform softly

ESSENTIAL ELEMENT #7: EXPRESSION

Let's take a look at the expression markings and experiment with ways to add them to your speeches so you can bring your words to life.

This works best when you say the sentence out loud, so you may want to move to a quiet place if other people are within earshot. The further away you move, the better.

Let's take a sentence you've heard repeatedly throughout your life:

If I told you once, I've told you 1,000 times...

Say the sentence using crescendo. This means you start the sentence quietly and reach peak volume on the last few words.

Now say the sentence using decrescendo. Start at your highest volume and gradually lower the volume so the last few words are spoken softly.

Can you feel the difference? Do you see how that would change the texture of the words?

We're not done yet. Have you moved further away from anyone nearby?

This time, I want you to say the whole sentence loud from beginning to end (forte).

Then do it softly (piano).

When you use expression in your speeches, you set yourself apart from the speaker who drones on in a monotone voice and masterfully cures insomnia, and you stand in stark contrast to the over-excited "motivational" speaker who is stuck on "yell" for his or her entire speech.

Oprah Winfrey is a master at using expression in her speeches. She does more than say words. She brings words to life and gives them value and meaning. To see this in action, watch her speech at the 2018 Golden Globe Awards show. Pay particular attention to the way she makes the word "strong" sound *strong*. And how she softens her voice on the phrase "like my mother." The words in the speech itself are powerful, but they become more powerful because of the way she masterfully navigates them.

Expression adds layers and texture that give life to your words and feeling to your speech. It allows you to play and experiment with what you say *and* how you say it.

You have my permission. Go ahead...express yourself.

Let's recap:

Expression in speeches is the use of dynamics, phrasing, timbre, and articulation to ensure you are not merely saying words but bringing those words to life. Some ways to add expression include

- Gradually getting louder
- Gradually getting softer
- Speak loudly
- Speak softly
- Crescendo or decrescendo on a single word

EXERCISE: EXPRESSION

Look back at the speech you've been working on and choose a passage to practice with. Using the methods of expression discussed in this chapter, experiment with the different ways you can use dynamics, volume, inflection, etc., to bring the words to life.

_____

_____

_____

_____

_____

One more to go! We've now covered seven of the eight essential elements that make a speech sound like music to their ears:

- Chorus
- Hook
- Verses
- Pre-chorus
- Mood
- Rhythm
- Expression

In the next chapter, we'll discuss Essential Element #8, the Bridge.

ESSENTIAL ELEMENT 8:
THE BRIDGE

The bridge serves two purposes:

1. To pause and reflect on the earlier portions of the song
2. To prepare the listener for the climax of the song and return to the chorus

In a speech, the lyrical bridge also serves two purposes:

1. To pause and summarize the main points of the speech
2. To prepare the audience for the climax of the speech and reinforce the chorus of the speech

To achieve the purposes I've listed, you can use one or a combination of the following closing strategies:

- Summarize key points
- Paint a picture of the future

- Talk about consequences
- Use a quotation
- Tell a story
- Use anaphora and epistrophe for emotional impact

SUMMARIZE KEY POINTS

It's been said "there's nothing new under the sun." There also shouldn't be any new points in your close. Repeat and review the key points you discussed earlier in your speech as a final reminder of the main points you want the audience to walk away with.

PAINT A PICTURE OF THE FUTURE

You don't have to be a futurist to paint a picture of the future. Just use your imagination and invite your listeners to join you. You don't even need to paint the picture yourself. Ask them what the future will look like a year from now if they do what you suggest...or if they decide not to.

TALK ABOUT CONSEQUENCES

What are the consequences of not following your advice? What about if your audience does follow your advice? Will there still be consequences?

Sometimes, taking positive action on your suggestions won't go as smoothly as you might make it sound. To be responsible and prepare your audience for real life, it's helpful to prepare people by talking about what could, and most likely will, happen once the lights go down and they go back to normal life.

USE A QUOTATION

In the chapter Essential Element #5, Mood, I provided several suggestions for different ways to use quotations at the start of your speech. Some of those suggestions won't apply here. For example, I don't recommend challenging a quote at the end of your speech. When you do it at the beginning, you're building your own credibility on the topic and giving audience members time to pause to think about your topic from a different point of view. When you use a quotation at the end of your speech, the purpose is to reinforce what you've already discussed and add more weight to your words. You should add very little, if anything at all, when you use a quote to close.

I often close my speeches this way:

> Dr. Myles Munroe once said..."Potential is all you can do but haven't done yet. All you can be, but haven't become yet. How far you can go, but haven't gone yet. And who you really are, but no one knows yet." I encourage you to keep striving to reach your potential.

TELL A STORY

As we discussed in Essential Element #3, the Verses, stories have the ability to help you and your audience members share an experience and feel connected emotionally. Whether you want to get them laughing, crying, or reminiscing about a special person in their life, closing with a story is powerful if done correctly.

Use Anaphora and Epistrophe for Emotional Impact

Although we covered anaphora and epistrophe in Essential Element #2, the Hook, it's important to return to them in this section. You see, the two rhetorical devices are the most powerful and effective when it comes to bringing your speech to a climactic moment.

If you want to excel at using them in your speeches, I highly recommend listening to political speeches.

Even if you're not a fan of politics, listening to political speeches is an excellent learning exercise. Just listening to a political speech will give you a feel for the way anaphora and epistrophe fit into the pattern of the lyrical bridge. Once you become accustomed to the pattern, it will become easier for you to replicate it in your speeches if you so choose.

A wonderful resource for political speeches can be found at www. AmericanRhetoric.com.

Just because I've listed the American Rhetoric site, don't be deceived into thinking anaphora and epistrophe are only used by American politicians. Winston Churchill also used the power of both rhetorical devices in his speeches. One of his most popular refrains is:

> **We shall fight** on the beaches, **we shall fight** on the landing grounds, **we shall fight** in the fields and in the streets...

This is not an exhaustive list of ways to close your speech, but the methods I've suggested are time-tested ways you should always consider using to end your speech on a powerful note.

Let's recap:

The bridge in a speech serves two purposes:

1. To pause and summarize the main points of the speech
2. To prepare the audience for the climax of the speech and reinforce the chorus

Some of the different methods you can use to close your speech include

- Summarize key points
- Paint a picture of the future
- Talk about consequences
- Use a quotation
- Tell a story
- Use anaphora and epistrophe for emotional impact

EXERCISE: BUILD THE BRIDGE

Review the speech you've prepared so far and decide which method(s) will work most effectively.

_____

_____

_____

Once you've determined which method(s) fit best, write out your close and read it out loud.

_____

_____

_____

You did it! We've covered all eight of the essential elements that make a speech sound like music to their ears:

- Chorus
- Hook
- Verses
- Pre-chorus
- Mood
- Rhythm
- Expression
- Bridge

In the next chapter, I'll share my final thoughts on how you can use everything we've covered to your advantage, and what you can do to sharpen your skills moving forward.

FINDING YOUR RANGE

Whenever I read a book on presentation skills, time management, leadership, or any topic that requires me to look differently at a topic or try something new, I find myself thinking:

I'm sure that works for them, but I'm not sure it would work for me.

I'm guessing you may have similar feelings after having read this book. You may be uncomfortable with some of the rhetorical devices or strategies I've presented. For one reason or another, something doesn't resonate with you and it wouldn't feel authentic for you to do it. If that's how you're feeling, good on you! It means you're aware of your range.

In music, singers have a vocal range. Range is the distance between the lowest note and the highest note a singer can reach. On the low end, think Barry White. On the high end, think Minnie Riperton or Mariah Carey. If you don't know who they are, check out videos of them on YouTube.

Although there are many ranges on the vocal scale, they're generally categorized as

- Soprano
- Alto
- Tenor
- Baritone
- Bass

I've listed them from high to low. Some vocalists have the ability to sing in more than one range. In any case, no one range is better than another. Each range has unique qualities about it that will be appreciated in different ways by different people.

The same can be said for speaking styles.

Jokes aren't meant for everyone to tell. Soaring rhetoric isn't the arena of every speaker. Tear-jerking stories aren't comfortable for everyone to share, and making statistics sing might seem to you like the equivalent of long fingernails scratching a chalkboard. You don't have to incorporate any methods you're not comfortable with.

By the same token, it's also quite possible you're uncomfortable with some of the things I've suggested because you haven't tried them before or often enough. You may try them and surprise yourself. You may have to try them multiple times before you realize the techniques work quite well for you. It's also possible multiple attempts will prove true what you felt in the first place. In any case, please try in a safe, supportive environment where you can receive feedback and guidance. One of the best ways to do that is seek out a local Toastmasters International club (www.toastmasters.org).

Once you become more comfortable and find your speaking range, challenge yourself to go deeper and become masterful at making your speeches sing. When you feel ready to challenge yourself more, stretch a little and try something new.

Speak in front of groups as often as you can and always seek to improve. Watch videos of yourself and pay attention to what you can do to make your words sing a little more sweetly.

Lastly, watch and listen to the successful speeches of the past and current speeches that cause a buzz. Because links on the internet change frequently, I won't add them in this book. You can, however, visit my website, www.johnwatkis.com/resources, to see my suggestions for speeches you should watch and listen to.

I wish you much success delivering speeches your audience will remember, repeat, and respond to, and I look forward to hearing how the Eight Essential Elements change your speeches.

I have all the confidence in the world you'll deliver speeches that sound like music to the ears of your audiences.

SUGGESTED RESOURCES

BOOKS
1. The Hero with a Thousand Faces (The Collected Works of Joseph Campbell), by Joseph Campbell
2. The Writer's Journey: Mythic Structure for Writers, by Christopher Vogler
3. The Story Formula: Mastering the art of connection and engagement through the power of strategic storytelling, by Kelly Swanson
4. Speaking of Funny: 77 Ways to Add Humor to Any Presentation, by David Glickman

WEBSITES
American Rhetoric, www.AmericanRhetoric.com
Vital Speeches of the Day, www.vsotd.com

STORYTELLING WORKSHOPS
Powerful Storytelling™, by Michel Neray, www.neray.com/keynotes

SPEAKING CLUBS
Toastmasters International, www.toastmasters.org

ABOUT THE AUTHOR

Born and raised in Toronto, Canada, John Watkis is a professional speaker, speaking performance coach, award-winning performer, and speechwriter. He's the first Canadian-born actor to play Mufasa in the Disney musical *The Lion King* and has spoken to thousands of participants throughout Canada, the United States, England, Wales, Australia, and Cyprus.

John uses his experience as a world-class performer to teach leaders how to deliver show-stopping speeches and presentations when they're called on to speak. His practical, easy-to-use techniques prove you don't have to be an entertainer to be entertaining.

To hire John for an upcoming event or to have him coach your executive team, contact him directly at (407) 488-9715 or by email at info@johnwatkis.com.